THE KNOWLEDGE OF
OUR LORD JESUS CHRIST

THE KNOWLEDGE OF OUR LORD JESUS CHRIST

By
Venerable Louis de Ponte, S.J.
(From the "Spiritual Guide")

Translated by a Religious of the Order of St Benedict

*This is eternal life, to know Thee the one true God,
and Jesus Christ whom Thou hast sent.—John 17:3*

CANA PRESS

NIHIL OBSTAT:
Eduardus J. Mahoney, S.T.D.
Censor deputatus

IMPRIMATUR:
Edm. Can. Surmont
Vicarius generalis

Westmonasterii, *die 23a Martii*, 1931

Originally Published by
Burns Oates and Washbourne Ltd., 1931

Newly revised and edited by Cana Press, 2022
CANA PRESS © 2022

All rights reserved

No part of this book may be reproduced or transmitted, in any form or by any means, without permission.

For information, address:
PO Box 85
Colebrook,
Tasmania, 7027,
Australia

notredamemonastery.org

ISBN
978-0-6454653-0-3

Contents

Chapter I
Of the perfect knowledge of our Lord Jesus Christ, which may be obtained by meditating on the book of His life. An abridgement of all that concerns His life and virtues.   1

    I. Of the mysteries of our Saviour according to His humanity   2

    II. Of the principal virtues of our Saviour   8

    III. Of the mysteries and perfections of Christ according to His Divinity   13

Chapter II
Of how hurtful it is to us to be ignorant of God and of Christ our Saviour; that perfect knowledge consists in a certain transformation of our spirit into the living image of His glory; how this transformation is effected and what are its excellences.   17

    I. Of this two-fold ignorance   18

    II. How to obtain a true knowledge of God and Jesus Christ   23

    III. Of the perfection and beauty to which this knowledge may ascend   29

Chapter III
That in the book of the life of Christ our Lord there are found seven things, in themselves very different, but here in a wonderful juxtaposition,

which should be diligently meditated upon with
due humility and charity. 35
    I. Of the manner in which we should meditate
on all these things 39
    II. Of the reasons for which our Lord has united
in His own Person things so contrary 44
    III. Of the affections which proceed from all
these things 47

Chapter IV

Of the knowledge of Christ our Lord in those things
which He did on His first entry into this world...
that is, in the mysteries of His Incarnation and His
Nativity. 53
    Incarnation and Nativity 53
    I. Of four virtues exercised by Christ our Lord
in the womb of His blessed Mother 54
    II. Of four other virtues which Christ our Lord
exercised at the time of His Nativity 60

Chapter V

Of the reading and meditation of the book of Jesus
Christ crucified.... Eight excellent properties of the
unitive love which shines forth from the Cross. 69
    I. How we may best profit by these three motives
in our meditations on the Passion 70
    II. Of the resemblance effected by love 75
    III. Of the mortification which love produces 79
    IV. Of the fortitude, both for action and for
suffering, which love engenders 82
    V. Of the generosity of love 86

Chapter VI

How we may acquire a loving knowledge of Jesus Christ in the Most Holy Sacrament, by the consideration of seven marvellous things contained in it; and of the heroic virtues He exercises therein and examples of perfection which He gives to all the faithful.   91

    I. Of the union of God and man with the species of bread and wine   94

    II. Of the miracle of transubstantiation, and how the accidents of bread and wine remain without the substance which naturally sustains them   97

    III. Of the manner in which Christ our Lord is present in this Sacrament   102

    IV. Of the coming of Christ our Lord into the Sacrament   105

Chapter VII

Of the love which unites us with Jesus Christ and with our neighbour, and which is an effect of the Sacrament of the Eucharist… of the different degrees of this union.   113

    I. Of the spiritual union of the soul with Jesus Christ   116
    II. Of the various degrees of this spiritual union   119
    III. Of the love which unites us with our neighbour   125
    IV. Of frequent Communion   131

Chapter VIII

That to the meditation of the mysteries of our Saviour ought to be joined mortification and imitation: in these three actions consists that spiritual commun-

ion which best disposes the soul for sacramental Communion. 135
   I. Of consideration 137
   II. Of mortification 139
   III. Of imitation 141
   IV. Of preparation for Communion 145

Chapter IX

Of the knowledge of Christ our Lord in the glory He has in heaven, and of what He is there doing for us. 149

Chapter X

Of that union with God by knowledge and love which is proper to the unitive way, and of its stupendous properties and effects. 161
   I. Of six properties belonging to the union wrought by charity 164
   II. Of six other wonders which accompany this union of love 169
   III. Of the manner in which knowledge and love effect the most intimate union between God and the soul 172

APPENDIX

Some Prayers from the "Meditations" 175
Spiritual Maxims 207

Chapter I

Of the perfect knowledge of our Lord Jesus Christ, which may be obtained by meditating on the book of His life. An abridgement of all that concerns His life and virtues.

THE MOST EXCELLENT BOOK, and the one most suited to the limitations of our human nature, in which to study the mystical science of the spirit and ascend to perfect contemplation, is Jesus Christ our Saviour, true God and true man, in whom is to be found all that is highest in God and all that is lowest in man; who said of Himself: *I am the door. By me, if any man enter in, he shall be saved: and he shall go in, and go out, and shall find pastures.*[1] By this He would have us know that He is indeed the only way that leads to salvation and eternal life, to fat and fertile pastures, in which the devout soul may always find wherewith to nourish and satisfy itself by the knowledge and love of divine things, by the exercise of virtues, by the abundance of graces and spiritual consolations with which it is filled. Let us then be fully persuaded that this is the gate by which we must enter in order to contemplate the mysteries of His Divinity and by which we must go out to consider those of His humanity. But it is also necessary that we should go in and out frequently, because it is impossible to take in at one glance all that is hidden in our Lord, and because we daily need fresh nourishment. For it will not suffice simply to regard His humanity if we do not penetrate to the divinity; to know well His divinity, we must first know His humanity. To believe with

[1] Jn 10:9

a firm faith all that regards these two things, to have a sure and loving knowledge of them, *this is eternal life*,[2] in this consists all our happiness; those who refuse to know them can never enter into Heaven: *Without faith,* by which we believe who God is and Christ is, *it is impossible to please God*[3] and attain salvation and the life of the spirit; and, as says St Peter: *there is no other name under Heaven given to men, whereby we must be saved,*[4] except the name of Jesus. For the just under the Old Law were saved by a living faith in the Saviour to come, although their faith was neither so clear nor so enlightened as ours.[5]

I. Of the mysteries of our Saviour according to His humanity

In order to put this matter in a clearer light,[6] let us premise that the life of Christ our Lord and His mysteries as described in the Gospels under the guidance of eternal Wisdom, is like that *book* which St John *saw in the right hand of Him that sat on the throne, written within and without,* folded like a scroll, and written on both sides; *sealed with seven seals… and no man was able, neither in Heaven nor on earth, nor under the earth, to open the book, nor to look on it, until the Lamb… standing as it were slain… came and took the book out of the right hand of Him that sat on the throne… and opened the book,*[7] breaking the seals. For the life of our Saviour is written in shining characters, which set forth His perfections and virtues: as it is written within and

[2] Jn 17:3
[3] Heb 11:6
[4] Acts 4:12
[5] St Thomas Aquinas, *Summa Theologiae*, IIa-IIae, q. 2, a. 7
[6] Cf. St Hilary, *Preface to the Psalter;* St Gregory, *Dialogues*, B. 4, ch. 42
[7] Apoc 5: 1, 3, 7

without, the interior declares His divinity and the exterior His humanity: we may also say that the interior represents His holy soul and the exterior His sacred body. But it is well to remark that the Man-God possesses nothing that He has not received from His Father, since His Father has communicated to Him by eternal generation all that is His as God, and by creation all that is His as man.

Before His Incarnation, this book was sealed with many seals, so that the faithful of the ancient law had only a confused knowledge of what is contained in its mysteries. Yet all were able to see these seven seals, they all had some knowledge of the prophecies, parables, sacrifices, ceremonies, sacraments, and of many wonderful events which happened in the days of their fathers, which were like figures and outlines of what would take place at the appointed time: but to interpret these mysteries, to explain these enigmas, it was necessary that the Lamb of God, the only-begotten Son of the Father, should descend from Heaven, and that the whole world should witness the actions of His life and the sorrows of His death. But at long last the shadows disappeared, the seals were broken, the mysteries were declared; of these the Church specially notes seven, in those seven articles of the Creed which concern the sacred humanity of our Saviour.[8]

The *first* seal was broken at the moment of the Incarnation, when this God of infinite majesty, whom neither Heaven nor earth can contain, was enclosed entire in the womb of a Virgin, took the form of an infant, clothed Himself in a body formed for Him by the Holy Spirit, and which He united to a soul into which He poured all the graces and virtues which the dignity of His Person demanded. Then the ancient prophecies began to find their fulfilment, and what had so long been hidden under the ancient figures was made manifest: so that we now know why the old seers had said that *a Virgin shall conceive and bear a*

[8] St Bernard, *Sermon on the Resurrection*

Son, and His name shall be called Emmanuel,[9] that is, God with us; and that *a woman shall compass a man*[10] in her womb; why *the Lord appeared* to Moses *in a flame of fire out of the midst of a bush,*[11]... which though on fire, *was not burnt*; why all the dew fell on the fleece;[12] why the *rod of Aaron budded* and *bloomed blossoms* and *formed almonds.*[13]

Nine months after the Incarnation the *second* seal was broken: the divine Infant was born in the stable at Bethlehem, without detriment to the virginity of His Mother; on the eighth day He was circumcised: then came the Magi to adore Him; He was presented in the Temple; He was carried away to Egypt; He returned to Nazareth, and there led a hidden life, admirable for its poverty, silence and humility.

When He reached the thirtieth year of His age, the *third* seal was opened, when, that is, He willed to manifest Himself to the world: beginning at His baptism when the heavens were opened and the Father and the Holy Spirit testified to His divinity and His sanctity, and soon after, as St Luke relates, *when He went into the synagogue on the sabbath day... and the book of Isaias,* till then closed, *was delivered unto Him. And as He unfolded the book, He found the place* which speaks of His entry into the world to preach the Gospel: He said to them all: *This day is fulfilled this scripture in your ears.*[14] And by those things which you have seen and heard you may know that the seal is taken away with which it was closed. During the years which followed He continued to preach His Gospel, and His preaching was accompanied by an infinite number of signs and

[9] Is 7:14; Mt 1:23
[10] Jer 31:22
[11] Ex 3:2
[12] Jg 6:37
[13] Num 17:8
[14] Lk 4:16, 17, 21

miracles; He never ceased to suffer horrible persecutions and inconceivable pain, until at last His enemies, jealous of His glory, having plotted His death, captured Him, scourged Him, crowned Him with thorns and nailed Him to a cross on which, before He expired, He tasted a little vinegar, that the Scripture might be fulfilled which had foretold this very thing: immediately after this He said: *It is consummated*,[15] that is, whatever was foretold and written of Me: moreover, all shall remain manifest and explained, in token of which the *veil of the Temple* which hid the Holy of Holies was *rent in two from the top even to the bottom*,[16] to signify that those mysteries which hitherto had been hidden under the veil of the law[17] were now unveiled, so that all the world might know and understand them.

At the moment of His death the *fourth* seal was removed: His blessed soul, always united with the Person of the Word, descended into limbo and even to the gates of Hell: it *penetrated*, says St Paul, *into the lower parts of the earth*;[18] and by virtue of its infinite merits, it drew out of these dark and gloomy regions an innumerable number of glorious captives.

On the third day the *fifth* seal was opened: this holy soul, returning to the sepulchre, was reunited to the body, and Jesus rose, full of glory, triumphant over death and sin, Hell and the prince of this world; He showed many infallible proofs of His resurrection: He opened the minds of His Apostles, that they might understand the Scriptures;[19] He explained them to them Himself, giving them the key, as St Luke tells us, and laying open before them ineffable mysteries which till then had not been explained.

[15] Jn 19:30
[16] Mt, 27:51
[17] Heb 9:8
[18] Eph 4:9
[19] Cf. Lk 24:27, 32, 45

During forty days He yet remained on earth, after which, desiring to break the *sixth* seal, He ascended to Heaven by His own power, taking with Him the train of captives whom He had released from limbo; each of these He placed according to His merits on the throne of glory which had been prepared for Him; but He Himself sat down at the right hand of His Father, with whom He has made Himself our advocate; from both Father and Son the Holy Ghost is sent down to us with all His stupendous gifts and graces, for the perfect conversion and sanctification of our souls.

This office He will continue to exercise till the last day of the world, when He will remove the *seventh* seal; even now we know much of what will happen on that terrible day, since the Judge Himself has declared to us in formal terms that He will come to judge the world with great glory and majesty;[20] that all the dead will rise; that He will separate the good from the wicked; on the former He will pronounce a favourable sentence, while the latter will be condemned; both decrees will immediately be carried out. He has told us of all these circumstances of His judgement, only hiding from us the knowledge of when it will be; this He has reserved to Himself alone. But when the great day shall come, all secrets will be disclosed: all men assembled in the valley of Jehosaphat will see the book wide open; the power and majesty of their Saviour will shine forth before their eyes for the confusion of the wicked and the joy of the good.

These are the seven principal mysteries regarding the sacred humanity of Christ our Lord, which were only known to men of old obscurely and veiled in figures, as one may see the cover of a book without being able to read what is written within. But we who live under the New Law, see them clearly and explicitly: for us they are no longer enigmas, the seals have been broken and the Saviour himself has fulfilled them all, as

[20] Mt 25:31 et seq

we have said. For by faith we believe and understand clearly and distinctly all that has been written and set down in the Gospels; by continual and assiduous meditation we ought to penetrate and make our own all that this book contains within and without: within we may study His divinity, without we contemplate His sacred humanity; we admire both the sufferings of His body and the excellent virtues of His soul; but we should apply ourselves to all this in vain, all our study would be useless if the Lamb of God Himself who, as we have said, is the only One who can open this book to His people, did not open it to each one of us individually and explain each mystery in particular: He will certainly do this for us if we put no obstacle in the way.

How much then does it behove us to realise and give thanks for the immense privilege which is ours, in that we have been born under the New Law, so that this book of the life and virtues of Christ our Lord is spread open for our reading and meditation. For *blessed,* said the Saviour Himself to his Apostles, *are your eyes, because they see what you see, and your ears because they hear* what you hear. *For, amen, I say to you, many prophets and just men have desired to see the things that you see, and have not seen them: and to hear the things that you hear and have not heard them.*[21] Since we also have obtained this grace, let us praise and give glory to Him who has bestowed such a benefit upon us. Let us never cease to bless Him, imitating the Ancients of the Apocalypse[22] who, *when He had opened the book… fell down before the Lamb having every one of them harps, and golden vials full of odours, which are the prayers of saints: and they sang a new canticle, saying: Thou art worthy, O Lord, to take the book, and to open the seals thereof; because Thou wast slain, and hast redeemed us to God, in Thy blood, out of every tribe and*

---

[21] Mt 13:16, Lk 10:23
[22] Apoc 5:8-13

tongue and people and nation; and hast made us to our God a kingdom and priests. And we shall reign on the earth. And I beheld, and I heard the voice of many angels round about the throne, and the living creatures, and the ancients (and the number of them was thousands of thousands) saying with a loud voice: The Lamb that was slain is worthy to receive power and divinity and wisdom and strength and honour and glory and benediction. Most sweet Saviour, I rejoice and exult with these Thy saints and heavenly hierarchies, I give thanks with them that Thou hast opened this admirable book and revealed to us the secret counsels of Thy eternal wisdom, and hast made plain for us all that was hidden under the types and figures of old. Enlighten me with Thy divine light that I may so read and understand it, that I may praise Thee in holy canticles and offer Thee fervent and fragrant prayers and the music of sweet affections. May I also come some day to enjoy the glorious kingdom and priesthood which Thou hast prepared for me, that I may reign with Thee and all Thy Saints in Thy eternal kingdom. Amen.

II. Of the principal virtues of our Saviour

All that we have said so far concerning Christ our Lord and the seven mysteries which regard His humanity may also be understood, in due proportion, of the virtues which He not only taught but practised and in which lie all the perfection of the Gospel law. This is another *book,* which, like the first, is *in the right hand* of God,[23] and of which Moses spoke, saying: *In His right hand a fiery law.*[24] It is *written within and without,* because it contains all those virtues which serve to adorn the interior man or to regulate the exterior, and because it prom-

[23] Apoc 5:1
[24] Deut 33:2

ises to the virtuous great rewards both in this life and the next. But before the coming of our Lord it was sealed with seven seals; for the many difficult and hard things it contained were the cause why men of old could neither read nor understand it: until Christ our supreme Master, coming into the world, opened the book and explained what was difficult, manifesting all these virtues first in Himself by example, and afterwards by His preaching; communicating also the grace of the Holy Spirit, by which their exercise was made easy.

This is clearly seen in the admirable discourse which He delivered upon the Mount when He opened His mouth that He might open and declare the heavenly doctrine shut up and concealed in this book; He began by exalting eight heroic virtues so hard and difficult to practise that until then they had been scarcely known to the world in the sense and manner in which He set them forth. And that His disciples might the better understand this, He immediately added: *You have heard that it was said to them of old: Thou shalt not kill... thou shalt not commit adultery... thou shalt not forswear thyself... thou shalt love thy neighbour and hate thy enemy. But I say to you*[25] that I will teach you another and a higher law of perfection, which until now has been shut up and closed to your fathers; therefore but few of them were perfect, and only one here and there attained to the practice of some of these virtues which I now mean to place within reach of all my disciples.

And although these virtues of which the Son of God speaks are many in number and of great excellence, yet they are all contained in what we call the eight Beatitudes, which correspond to the seven seals of our book. For although, says St Thomas,[26] there are eight, yet the eighth is contained in the other seven, and so to eight virtues there are allotted only seven rewards.

---

[25] Mt 5:21 et seq.
[26] St Thomas Aquinas, *Summa Theologiae*, Ia-IIae, Q. 69, art. 3, ad 5

First then, He unfastened the seal of *poverty,* saying: *Blessed are the poor in spirit, for theirs is the kingdom of Heaven.*[27] And what was there in the whole world more hidden and unknown than the beatitude concealed in the renunciation of all things, in casting out of the heart all affection for them, and distributing them, if need be, to the poor? And who is He who says that blessedness consists in abnegation of self and the renunciation of honours and renown, choosing always for oneself the lowest place? It is the Lamb of God, Jesus Christ himself, who has laid open for us what was shut up and sealed in this book concerning true perfection and sanctity, being made poor and lowly for us and teaching His disciples the same poverty and humility which He Himself embraced, that they might imitate Him: for in them He promised that they should find perfection and beatitude both temporal and eternal.

Next He breaks the seal of *meekness,* saying: *Blessed are the meek, for they shall possess the land;* by declaring this He shows how we ought to repress every motion of anger, not only that which is outward, but also inward, avoiding all contention, bearing contempt, condoning injuries and offering ourselves rather to endure fresh ones than to avenge those we have already received: so that *if one strike thee on thy right cheek, turn to him also the other* that he may strike that too; *and if a man will… take away thy coat, let go thy cloak also unto him.*[28] choosing rather to suffer the loss of temporal things than to turn aside ever so little from true sanctity and justice.

Then He opens the *third* seal, saying: *Blessed are they that mourn, for they shall be comforted;* for true consolation does not consist in laughing and joking, as the world thinks, but in grieving over our sins and doing penance for them: chastising the flesh and compelling it to enter the narrow gate of morti-

[27] Mt 5:3
[28] Mt 5:39, 40

fication; forcing it to bear the cross and, if need be, die upon it. And lest we should do this with any sadness or disgust, He opened the *fourth* seal, saying: *Blessed are they that hunger and thirst after justice,* esteeming their food and drink to be obedience to God and the fulfilment of His law, shouldering the burdens and obligations of their state of life and treading their own will under foot. In so doing they carry out the will of God and of His ministers, finding all their joy in such obedience, as one who is hungry and thirsty delights in taking food and drink; they also do the will of God as perfectly as it is done in Heaven. Hence He passes to the *fifth* seal, saying: *Blessed are the merciful,* and later He mentions in great detail the various works of mercy, temporal as well as spiritual, towards all our neighbours, extending them even to our enemies, that is, doing good to those from whom we receive evil, blessing those who curse us and honouring those who calumniate and persecute us: in this we shall become merciful and perfect, as our heavenly Father is perfect, who does good alike to the good and the bad, the just and the unjust.

After this He comes to the *sixth* seal, namely, cleanness of heart, saying: *Blessed are the clean of heart;* laying down that this cleanness ought to reach such a heroic degree that neither in work, word nor thought should we ever admit anything which can stain it; and that this may be the more perfectly attained, He would have us extend it to cleanness of body also: namely, renouncing all carnal pleasures, not merely those which are forbidden but even many which are lawful, so that while still living in this mortal flesh we may lead a life angelic in its purity, and become worthy even to see God, enjoying on earth that sweet contemplation which we shall only possess in its full perfection and delight in Heaven.

Lastly He opens the *seventh* seal, which is the fruit of that charity which belongs to the sons of God: *Blessed,* He says, *are the peacemakers: for they shall be called the children of God;* here He teaches us that happiness consists in perfect union and peace and concord with God Himself and with our neighbour; and in doing all that lies in us to keep our neighbours also at peace with God and among themselves, loving each other in God; and lastly, in desiring to see the glory of God more and more promoted and the mystical body of Christ, which is His Church, grow daily in sanctity and perfection.

But because in the practice of these virtues we are sure to meet with many and great contradictions, He concludes by saying: *Blessed are they who suffer persecution for justice' sake*, namely, in preserving that virtue and sanctity of which we have spoken, so that if they persevere in it patiently and constantly, they shall be assured of the possession of the kingdom of Heaven and fully enjoy the promised reward.

These are the principal virtues written in the book of the life of Christ our Lord and which He Himself first brought to light, practising them from the time of His Nativity in the cave at Bethlehem until His death upon the cross: there is not one of which we do not find admirable examples in His life, according to the prophecy of Isaias, to whom God, speaking of His only-begotten Son, said: *Take thee a great book* (the Septuagint calls it *great* and *new) and write in it with a man's pen*[29] all which is about to happen. By this He would signify that His most holy Son was to be made like to a kind of book, great and new: great in His sanctity, new in His manner of practising it; which was to be written with the perfect pen of a man, that is in characters so clear and distinct and glorious that all men, from the greatest to the least, should be able to read and understand it, and accomplish without difficulty all that it teaches; from it we may learn in what the virtues of true perfection and sanctity consist, and so may be conformed to what we have read in this divine book.

[29] Is 8:1

And because of our great good fortune in having this book open before us, it ought to be our principal study daily to read and meditate upon it; striving to understand, ruminate and imitate each and every one of the virtues, both interior and exterior, and the rewards which are apportioned to them: as we have already described in speaking of each of the eight Beatitudes in its place and afterwards shall speak more fully concerning them.

Let us not pass over in silence what St Jerome remarks, that the prophet Isaias, when about to write in the aforesaid book with a man's pen, *took to himself two faithful witnesses, Urias,* which signifies the light, or fire of the Lord, and *Zacharias,* which means the memory of God. What else does this signify, but that in order to meditate as we ought on the life and virtues of our Saviour, we have need of light from Heaven and the Holy Spirit, with the remembrance of the presence of God? For by this light we understand what we read and meditate on, and by this fire desire is enkindled of imitating it and carrying it out in our actions; the memory of the presence of God will make us diligently attend to what we are about. Saviour of the world, who art at once book and Master, helper and witness, light and fire, be present to me while I read and meditate on Thy mysteries and virtues; occupy my memory, enlighten my mind and inflame my will, that I may understand what I read, love what I understand, and carry out in deeds what I love. Amen.

III. *Of the mysteries and perfections of Christ according to His Divinity*

We have still much to say of the sublime and excellent things which Christ our Saviour has revealed to us concerning His divinity and His infinite perfections. For of His divinity also it may be said that it is a book written within and without but signed with seven seals with regard to many hidden and admirable things which were not explained under the old law: neither should we comprehend them now, if Jesus Christ, the Lamb of God, had not by opening the book revealed them to us, according to that saying of the Evangelist concerning Him: *No man hath seen God at any time: the only-begotten Son who is in the bosom of the Father, He hath declared Him.*[30]

And although He has revealed to us many mysteries, some which pertain to the Divinity itself; others to those external operations which proceed from it: yet all may be summed up in those seven mysteries or articles placed before us by the Church in her *Credo*. First, He opened the seal of His eternal generation, revealing to us that God is truly the Father of infinite majesty, self-existent, the principle from which all else proceeds. Second, this Father, before all ages, by an act of His intelligence produced the divine Word, who is His Son. Third, that the Holy Spirit proceeds eternally from the Father and the Son, as from one same principle, by an act of Their will, that is to say, by Their mutual love for each other. Fourth, that although there are really three distinct Persons, They are all one in essence; They are in very truth but one only God, equal in eternity, in goodness, and in all other attributes; so that none is more ancient, more holy, more wise or more powerful than the other. Fifth, in consequence, They are most perfectly united in all Their operations; having the same lights, designs, and powers They always act in concert without any possibility of division between Them; thus in all three, we should adore but one Creator, one Preserver and one only Master of the world. Sixth, that the Blessed Trinity has manifested an admirable providence in regard to mankind in the means of redemption through the Incarnation of the Son, in which all three Persons showed forth Their infinite charity and mercy, joined to sov-

[30] Jn 1:18

ereign justice. For the Father could not show us greater love than by giving us His only-begotten Son to redeem us; nor could the Son manifest greater commiseration in our regard than by taking upon Himself the penalty due to our sins. For His justice could not condone our faults until an adequate satisfaction had been made for them: since man could not do this, He became man Himself that He might pay the debt man owed. But this satisfaction would have been without fruit had not the Holy Spirit Himself descended invisibly on men to carry out the work of sanctification: for He goes before us with His holy inspirations, He enriches us with His grace, He communicates to us His gifts, He strengthens our faith, He teaches us to pray and excites us to the practice of all virtues, conferring upon us with the utmost liberality all His treasures of divine grace. Seventh, and lastly, we believe that this same God who has saved us will be the glorious reward of His elect; opening Heaven to them all and admitting them to the clear vision of His own divinity: by this shall they be blessed as He is blessed, and enjoy the very same happiness as He enjoys.

These are the seven mysteries which our Saviour Himself has revealed to us; they ought to serve us as matter for meditation and contemplation with fervent desires of knowing and loving this great God, three in one, and of emulating, as far as in us lies, His virtues. But let us notice that it was with many tears that the Evangelist St John implored the Lamb, whom he saw before him, to open the book that he might read and understand it: *And no man was able, neither in Heaven, nor on earth, nor under the earth, to open the book: neither* was anyone found worthy *to look on it;*[31] do thou also confess that the Saviour alone can give thee a true knowledge and appreciation of these profound mysteries, neither canst thou, nor any other creature search them out for himself; with tears and

[31] Cf. Apoc 5:3

sighs therefore, supplicate Him to open them for thee and unfold their meaning to thy spirit: otherwise they will remain closed and veiled to thee. Lamb of God, who holdest *the key of David, and what Thou openest, no man shutteth; what Thou shuttest, no man openeth;*[32] humbly I implore Thee that with the key of Thy divine knowledge Thou wilt open for me Thy sublime mysteries, that I may understand and assimilate their true meaning, and by their means attain to that end for which Thou hast opened them to us. Amen.

---

[32] Apoc 3:7

Chapter II

Of how hurtful it is to us to be ignorant of God and of Christ our Saviour; that perfect knowledge consists in a certain transformation of our spirit into the living image of His glory; how this transformation is effected and what are its excellences.

ALTHOUGH CHRIST OUR LORD, as we have said, has opened this book and disclosed all that is contained in it, speaking to us in so plain and familiar a manner that anyone who with lively faith desires *to read it, may run over it*[1] without fear of danger, yet there are still many who cannot read it, but it remains as dark to them as if it had never been unsealed: such persons labour under a twofold and very grave ignorance, first of Christ the Saviour of the world, and secondly, of *God Himself*[2] mingling many errors with what they have learnt concerning them. Their misery was deplored by the Apostle, saying: *O senseless Galatians, who hath bewitched you that you should not obey the truth, before whose eyes Jesus Christ hath been set forth,*[3] and the sentence of condemnation to death which is hidden in the Scripture? or, as St John Chrysostom says, who have Christ before you, like a writing or picture, in which you may read the truth of His Gospel. How full the world is of these foolish people, who seem to be bewitched and as if absorbed in the pleasures of this life and have no eyes for heavenly mysteries! But what wonder is it if a miserable man, who has nothing nearer

[1] Hab 2:2
[2] Cf. 1 Cor 15:34
[3] Gal 3:1

to him than his own self, and yet is ignorant of his own misery, should add to this the misery of ignorance of his Creator and his Saviour? For if it is, as we have said, a great evil to be ignorant of oneself, how much more hurtful will it be not to know Him who has drawn us out of nothing, and who will be our eternal happiness? *If any man know not,* says the Apostle,[4] *he shall not be known;* as if he would say: he who knows not God and Jesus Christ, shall not be known by Them, that is with the knowledge of approval, by which the elect are known; nay rather, at the last day He will say to them: *I know you not.*[5] For as *this is eternal life: That they may know* well *God and Jesus Christ whom He has sent:*[6] so will it be eternal death not to be known but to be ignored by Them. For from this come innumerable evils and sins, as the Lord Himself has said: *All the earth is laid waste... for My foolish people have not known Me;*[7] and *therefore is My people led away captive, because they had not knowledge.*[8] For although they may have many other kinds of knowledge, if this is wanting to them it is the same as if they had none. For by this ignorance are they led away captive by their enemies the devils, they are bound by the chains of their own sins, caught in the net of their own passions, and cast out of the promised land, which is the Church, into the Babylon of eternal confusion, which is Hell.

I. *Of this two-fold ignorance*

But because our misery is so great that we are unable to realise the depth of our ignorance, it is well to notice that this

[4] 1 Cor.14:38
[5] Mt, 25:12
[6] Cf. Jn 17:3
[7] Jer 4:20, 22
[8] Is 5:13

ignorance or error concerning God and our Lord Christ is of two kinds: the one speculative, the other practical.

The first of these is detrimental to faith, because it hinders us from believing some truth which faith teaches, or else it makes us believe some error which is contrary to what has been revealed to us concerning God and Christ our Lord. Such is the ignorance under which Jews and Turks labour who, although they do not make for themselves, as do the heathen, gods of silver and gold, which are the images of their false deities, yet in their own minds they form thoughts and concepts which are not images of the true God or the true Christ, our Saviour, but vain representations of an imaginary God or an imaginary Christ, fashioned out of their own ignorance. For they represent to themselves a God who is not a pure spirit, or who is not three Persons, or who has no providence for His creatures; or a Christ who is man only and not God, or who has not a body which is real but only a phantom: all these are in truth idols, since there does not exist in the world such a God or such a Christ as those which they imagine.

Hence it is that they contemn the true God, of whom they are ignorant because, as says the holy Apostle St Jude: *these men blaspheme whatever they know not;*[9] they deny whatever they do not understand and speak against that which they neither believe nor know. And even till the present day Christ our Lord, as the prophet Isaias foretold, is as the words of a book that is sealed[10] to multitudes who have not the faith. The mysteries of His infancy, His life, His passion and His death seem to them so unworthy of the majesty of God that they cannot believe that one whom they see so utterly humiliated is truly God. This is the lot of the Jews who formed for themselves a concept of the Messias for whom they hoped, which was full

[9] Jude 10
[10] Is 29:11

of innumerable errors. They pictured Him to themselves as a temporal king, wealthy, powerful and warlike; but when they saw the Christ so poor, humble and abject, they could not recognise in Him the Messias, and, moreover, cast Him out and crucified Him.

But setting aside such people who are without God and without Jesus Christ, against whose ignorance many other books have been written, let us come to another kind of ignorance and error in practice which is that of many of the faithful, of whom St Paul said: *They profess that they know God: but in their works they deny him.*[11] St John also says: *He who saith that he knoweth* God, *and keepeth not His commandments, is a liar, and the truth is not in him.*[12] And again: *Whosoever sinneth, hath not seen Him nor known Him,*[13] because he has not known Him as he ought; he does not think of Him such as He truly is, but has of Him only a slight and confused notion, and the idea of God which he has formed for himself is utterly unworthy of the greatness and extent of His divine perfections. St Bernard,[14] treating of this subject with great lucidity, says that hardened sinners are in a profound ignorance with regard to God; for what is it which hinders them from conversion and from returning to Him except that they regard as too severe Him who is infinitely good; as pitiless, Him who is full of mercy; as cruel and angry, Him who is loving and charitable? Thus, in the words of the Psalmist: *Iniquity hath lied to itself,*[15] it imposes upon itself when it puts false deities in the place of the true God, since there cannot be found in the whole world a God like to the one they have fashioned for themselves.

---

[11] Tit 1:16
[12] 1 Jn 2:4
[13] *Ibid.*, 3:6
[14] Sermon 38 *on the Canticle*
[15] Ps 26:12

Such was the ignorance and error of that slothful servant who buried the talent and hid the money of his lord, and when the time came for giving in his account, showed what was his opinion of his master by saying: *Lord, I know that thou art a hard man; thou reapest where thou hast not sown, and gatherest where thou hast not strewed. And being afraid, I went and hid thy talent in the earth: behold here thou hast that which is thine.*[16] In the same way, sinners, the lukewarm and the imperfect imagine, for themselves, each one according to their own fancy, God and Jesus Christ. To the scrupulous, God seems to be severe, difficult to please and ready to exact the last farthing; one who is over-anxious thinks God indifferent and slow in coming to his aid, because he is not immediately relieved from the cause of his worry; the fainthearted depict Him as inexorable, severe in His judgements, already prompt to revenge an injury; the soft and self-indulgent make Him too merciful, and say: *The mercy of the Lord is great, He will have mercy on the multitude of my sins,*[17] trusting to find repentance on their death-bed.

During His lifetime on earth, the Jews held many different opinions concerning the personality of Christ our Lord; for *some* thought Him to be *John the Baptist,* others *Elias,* and others *Jeremias, or one of the prophets:*[18] so now each one depicts Christ according to his own fancy. Some represent Him as austere and solitary, like John the Baptist, persuading themselves that the only way to salvation lies in penance and solitude: others would make Him like to Elias, whose ardent zeal brought down fire from Heaven to consume sinners; they imagine Him with the lightning ready in His hand and that He revenges Himself immediately for every injury. This error He Himself

[16] Mt, 24:18, 24-25
[17] Cf. Ecc 5:6
[18] Mt 16:14

showed to be utterly opposed to His true spirit when He said to the two over-zealous disciples: *You know not of what spirit you are.*[19] Others imagine Christ our Lord to resemble Jeremias, always weeping and lamenting, as if the spirit of Christ was one of continual tears and sadness: such people think that anyone who has once sinned could never be joyful again.

Such false conceptions as these, besides many others, obsess many men, not that Christians really in their heart of hearts believe such things of Christ and God, but they behave just as if they did do so: from this it arises that some are wanting in confidence, while others presume, some are negligent and others scrupulous: in consequence these are all out of the right way and all have false ideas of God and Jesus Christ.

Similar errors are also to be met with regarding the nature and merits of the Christian virtues. It is an axiom of the Philosopher[20] that whoever sins is ignorant, and the Wise Man says: *They err that work evil;*[21] their error consists principally in this, that they have too little esteem for the goodness, justice and sanctity of God, and that they do not sufficiently realise how detestable sin is.[22] Again, their estimation of the law of God is very erroneous, especially concerning the recompense of virtue and the punishment of vice, because they are either ignorant or understand very confusedly how easy and light are the precepts of the divine law, how sweet are the delights of Heaven, how insupportable the pains of Hell. To dispel these illusions, it is most important that we should exercise ourselves diligently in reading and meditating all that is written in the book of the most glorious life and doctrine of the Saviour our Lord, as He Himself has revealed and declared them: for He

---

[19] Lk 9:55
[20] Aristotle, 3 Ethic., c. 1
[21] Prov 14:22
[22] St Thomas Aquinas, ST. I-II, Q. 76, art. 4, ad 1 et Q. 78, art. 1, ad 1

has depicted Himself in this book; in it also He has given us a true portrait of His Father; He has pointed out distinctly all those virtues without which it is impossible to glorify and serve Him, in order that we may know clearly what we ought both to love and imitate.

II. How to obtain a true knowledge of God and Jesus Christ

A sure and direct means of learning to know God and Jesus Christ his Son, is taught us by St Paul: *We all*, he says, *beholding the glory of the Lord with open face, are transformed into the same image from glory to glory, as by the Spirit of the Lord.*[23] For by the glory of the Lord he means those mysteries in which have shone forth most resplendently the glory of one God in three Persons and the glory of Jesus Christ, who is the splendour of the substance[24] of the Eternal Father, with all those graces and gifts and virtues which are manifested in that divine book of which we have spoken. These, says the Apostle, we of the new covenant may contemplate in a manner unknown to those who lived under the old dispensation. For the children of Israel, being dazzled by the brightness of the face of Moses, could only behold him when covered with a veil; and even till the present day, the Jews can only look upon the mysteries of Christ as it were through a veil, amidst the shadows of the Law; for He is to them still a sealed book. Their hearts are yet wrapped up in that veil which typifies their blindness, incredulity and ignorance: they have read the Scriptures, but they are content with the letter without caring to penetrate to the hidden meaning. But we gaze upon these mysteries with *open face,* the veil being taken away and the seals removed in the

[23] 2 Cor 3:18
[24] Cf. Heb 1:3

holy Gospels;[25] in them, as in a polished mirror, we behold the reflection of Christ our Lord; we follow Him through the different phases of the life He lived for us and we endeavour to imitate His example; we become transformed into Him, and by the grace of the Holy Spirit, rising from glory to glory, we are filled with His divine brightness.

In speaking thus the Apostle teaches us, as it were by the way, the qualities of spiritual men who are given to prayer and contemplation and in what they differ from tepid persons who have neither relish nor esteem for these exercises. Carnal souls always see spiritual things through a veil or mist which hides the mysteries of faith from their sight; at best they may be said to look into a mirror covered with dust or vapour: in it they cannot see distinctly what is reflected, but only confusedly or dimly. The multitude of their passions weakens their faith, their reason is blinded by brutal passions, the infrequency of their meditations on the truths of faith prevents their understanding them. Hence it is that they are content to believe them in general, without troubling to acquire a particular knowledge of those things which concern God and Jesus Christ, Hell and Heaven; having therefore only a very superficial knowledge of these things, their hearts are scarcely touched at all and they make no effort to become transformed into God, nor to reduce to practice what their faith teaches them.

Spiritual persons, on the contrary, contemplate divine things as in a very clear mirror, which shows them such as they truly are and hides nothing from them: they understand them as if they actually saw them with their eyes, and since they are animated by a lively faith accompanied by extreme purity of heart, they are able to form a very distinct concept of them. When therefore they consider the Son of God as if annihilated

[25] *Speculari est in speculo videre.* St Thomas Aquinas, Lect. 2 et 2, Q. 180, art. 3, ad 4

in a mortal body, they are in no wise ashamed to see Him thus abased: far from being covered with confusion at His insults, they regard them with joy and cease not to glorify Him, not only for the great things which He has revealed concerning His divinity, but also for those humiliating things which He has done and suffered in the eyes of the world according to His humanity. For it is to both these that they believe St John to refer when he said: *We saw His glory, the glory as it were of the only-begotten of the Father, full of grace and truth.*[26] They remember that when He was born in a stable, the angels sang: *Glory to God in the highest,*[27] because they beheld His magnificence and His virtues resplendent amidst the feebleness of infancy and the obscurity of a stable.

For this reason they make it all their glory to imitate Him,[28] to live poor and unknown as He was, and they prefer His cross to all that the world holds most glorious. So also, when they meditate on the mysteries of His life, the principal end they set before themselves, according to St Paul, is to transform themselves into His image, that is, to replenish themselves with His lights and virtues, just as the iron in the furnace so far takes on the colour and other qualities of fire that its own nature seems to be changed. This is how just souls, by contemplating the divinity and humanity of Christ, are transformed into His divine image;[29] by dint of considering His light, His beauty, His sanctity, they put on His likeness and their soul becomes so adorned with heavenly graces, gifts and virtues that one might say they live no longer, but God and Jesus Christ live in them.[30] And just as this Lord clothed Himself in various differ-

[26] Jn 1:14
[27] Lk 2:14
[28] Cf. Gal 6:14
[29] Cf. St Bonaventure, De tert. grad., cont., tom, 2
[30] Gal 2:12

ent forms, in the crib, on Mount Tabor and Mount Calvary: so into all these does the just man desire to be transformed, rising *from glory to glory;* not as if he could effect this transformation himself, but as the Apostle says: *as by the Spirit of the Lord;* for this is the work of the divine Spirit only, they co-operating to the utmost of their power, as we are about to see.

In the first place, let us suppose that the human mind is like a painter who is occupied all day making portraits and effigies of all those things visible or invisible which come to his notice; these images are called concepts. Now these concepts are nothing else than thoughts, because the moment we think of some object, we form in our mind a kind of picture which represents it in the state in which we perceive it. So St John says that when in Heaven God *shall appear, we shall be like to Him; because we shall see Him as He is;*[31] by this he means that the beatific Vision is a kind of clear similitude of God, portrayed upon our soul, by which we shall become like Him. But as painters who are not skilful do not always succeed with their portraits, which sometimes do not in the least, or very little, resemble the person whom they wished to present: so when ignorant persons think of God and Jesus Christ, their mind can only form in itself a false or very imperfect image. It is only spiritual persons who are given to prayer who are capable of forming a true likeness and who conceive of the divine perfections as they truly are in themselves and as they are depicted in the Holy Scriptures.

This is symbolised in the Bride of the Canticle who, being asked what her Spouse is like, forthwith depicts him and describes all his rare qualities in great detail: *My Beloved, she says, is white and ruddy, chosen out of thousands. His head is as the finest gold: his locks as branches of palm trees, black as a raven. His*

[31] 1 Jn 3:2

eyes as doves upon brooks of waters, which are washed with milk;[32] and so she continues, going through all the parts of his body, showing by all these similitudes how exactly she knew all his perfections and virtues. After this manner, therefore, oughtest thou to endeavour to form within thyself by reading and meditation a certain concept and idea of what God and Jesus Christ are in Themselves. That is, of Their goodness, charity, wisdom, patience and the other virtues and perfections which our faith teaches us; conceiving a very high opinion of Them so that thou mayest impress Their image on thine own mind, and that this image may be like to what has been revealed about Them in the Holy Scriptures; by this knowledge thou mayest begin to be transformed into the image of Their glory.

But this will not of itself produce the transformation. For from this image which is imprinted on the mind ought to proceed another, depicted on our very heart; we must imitate the virtues of our supreme Lord, we must have the same sentiments as He has, and as far as possible, we must become perfect, as He is perfect.[33] If therefore we have portrayed for ourselves in our own mind a God holy, charitable and merciful, a Jesus Christ poor, humble, weeping in the crib or expiring on the cross, we must necessarily have the same image imprinted on our will. By this means we shall come to perform works like to those of our Saviour; we shall accomplish what He commands when He says: *Put me as a seal upon thy heart, as a seal upon thy arm.*[34] It is not without deep mystery that He compares Himself to the figure which is graven upon a seal, for it serves not merely to please the eyes or to bring to the memory the person whom it represents: its principal use is to reproduce its own likeness on the object to which it is applied, in order that

---

[32] Cant 5:10-12
[33] Mt 5:48
[34] Cant 8:6

one may know to whom it belongs, and that it may be preserved with greater care. In the same way the living image and idea of Jesus Christ our Lord, which is placed before us in our reading and meditation, serves not only to console us and to bring to our memory all that we read and meditate concerning Him, but also to reproduce in us all His features, in order that we may be entirely conformed to His likeness both interiorly and exteriorly. For He has, moreover, said that we are to place this seal both upon our heart and upon our arm. By the heart, says Theodoret,[35] is understood that contemplative life which is entirely interior, and which consists in acts of the mind and will: the arm designates the active life, which is occupied in exterior works. In the Old Law God had commanded[36] the priests to take for their portion the breast and right shoulder of the victim; by this they were to understand that their whole lives were to be passed in the interior works of the contemplative life joined with the exterior labours of the active life. So when Jesus says to us: Put Me as a seal upon your heart and upon your arm, He admonishes us to imprint His divine image upon our intellect, so that we may know Him, on our heart that we may love Him, on our senses and all our powers; that we make it all our happiness to know, love and imitate Him; that we make ourselves like Him both within and without; that we receive His image as the wax receives that of the seal, and that thus transformed entirely into Him we may be able, as says the Apostle, to pass *from glory to glory*.[37] From the glory, namely, of Jesus Christ to our own glory and from the glory of knowledge to the glory of love, and thence to the glory of works: thus all will be glorified by the image of this divine seal. Beloved of my soul, Thou dost command me to put Thee like

---

[35] *Vide* Martin del Rio hic
[36] Ex 29:26, 27
[37] *A claritate in claritatem*

a seal upon my heart and my arm; but suppliantly I implore Thee that Thou wilt put Thyself as a seal upon my whole spirit with all its powers, for this Thou knowest I cannot do without Thee; put Thyself therefore as a seal upon all my faculties, imprinting upon them Thy image as Thou truly art, that I may know, love and imitate Thee, that I may be transformed into Thee and that Thou mayest live in me for all eternity. Amen.

III. Of the perfection and beauty to which this knowledge may ascend

But who can declare the manner in which Christ our Lord fulfils this desire of impressing Himself as a seal upon our spirit? He Himself has declared it, speaking to His eternal Father: *The glory which Thou hast given to Me, I have given to them; that they may be one, as We also are one: I in them, and Thou in Me; that they may be made perfect in one,* and be perfected by this union: *that the world may know that Thou hast sent Me, and hast loved them, as Thou hast also loved Me.*[38] Oh, the height of the charity of Christ! Could it possibly ascend higher than to impart to His elect that glory which He Himself has received from His eternal Father? And in what does this glory consist except in the glory of knowledge and love, with those glorious gifts which accompany them? But it is given to us by God himself; unless He gave it, we could never attain to it by our own power; He puts Himself as a seal upon our spirit, that He may impress its image upon it so exactly that we may become one with Him, as says the Apostle: *He who is joined to the Lord is one spirit,*[39] that is, with His spirit: so that by this resemblance the world may know the excellence of that Lord whose seal

[38] Jn 17:22, 23
[39] 1 Cor. 6:17

we bear, and may believe that the Father has sent Him to be the Master, Redeemer and Exemplar of all. He has broken the seven seals of external ceremonies and figures, with which the book was closed and sealed to the Hebrew people, and in their place He has willed to be Himself the seal of the book of His most glorious life, with which the Christian people are signed, impressing upon His elect the living image of His life: *that the life of Jesus,* as says the Apostle, *may be made manifest in their bodies,*[40] that they may be armed and protected by it, until they pass to that heavenly country where they will attain perfect union in the beatific vision.

But let us now see how far this resemblance may go in this life; may it be so perfect that the just man may become one with God as the Father and the Son are one, so that God and himself may be, so to say, but one same thing. *I am the Good Shepherd,* said Jesus Christ to the Jews, *I know My sheep and Mine know Me. As the Father knoweth Me, and I know the Father.*[41] Let us now see in what manner the Father knows the Son, and how the Son knows the Father and the sheep of His flock. Our faith teaches us that the Eternal Father, knowing His own divine essence, by that knowledge produces a living and infinite image of Himself, namely, His only-begotten Son, Whom for this reason we call the Word and the wisdom of the Father. This Word the Father has brought forth from all eternity, communicating to Him His divinity and all His perfections with such resemblance that both are one same thing in essence; and that with such joy and love that it is not possible He should not please and delight Himself in Him and love Him with an infinite love; by Him also He does all things, since they have but one same will and operation. It is after this manner therefore that this good shepherd, Christ Jesus,

[40] 2 Cor 4:10
[41] Jn 10:14, 15

knows His chosen sheep, with an all-embracing knowledge, benevolent and efficacious, impressing upon them the image and likeness of His divine nature, that is, His grace and charity, with the other virtues and supernatural gifts; He is united and joined to them like a seal, receiving them as His own and loving and delighting Himself in them, and working through them things most glorious.

In this manner then, not equally, but in due proportion, those perfect disciples of Christ who are the most valuable sheep of His flock come to Him, that they may know Him with a certain knowledge so strong and efficacious that they form in their own minds a kind of image of Christ Himself with His virtues and perfections, pleasing and delighting themselves in them; in the same lifelike and efficacious manner they imprint them upon their will, loving their Shepherd and taking Him for their own, joining themselves to Him, neither desiring to do or work anything except with Him, for Him and following in His footsteps, so that they say with the Apostle: *I live; now not I, but Christ liveth in me.*[42] I live a natural life, but He lives in me a supernatural life; my knowledge, my love, my affections and my deeds all proceed from Him, are referred to Him, by Him I do them and He in me: because we are one Spirit. He is in me and I in Him by love. In the same manner Christ Himself, as man, knows His Father with a knowledge of benevolence, fulfilling most exactly His divine will, imitating His perfections, approving what He disposes, carrying it out at the smallest sign, so that the image of infinite perfection which He has received from His Father, as God, He impresses upon Himself as man, with unspeakable similarity; on which account, in its own degree, we may say that what the Father is, such is the Son, and that *He who seeth the Son, seeth the Father also.*[43]

[42] Gal 2:20
[43] Jn 14:9

Eternal Father, who hast *predestinated Thy elect to be made conformable to the image of Thy Son*,[44] suppliantly I implore Thee through Him to grant me this favour: to know Him, to love Him, and so to imitate Him in spirit that I may be wholly conformed and transformed into the image of His glory. Most dear Redeemer who, whilst Thou wert praying upon Mount Tabor, didst transform and transfigure Thy body into the glorious likeness of Thy soul, and didst transform Moses and Elias into the image of Thine own glory and majesty:[45] transform and transfigure my soul into Thine, impressing upon it the figure of Thy excellent virtues, so that by their likeness I may be made one with Thee. Amen.

In order that we may more easily attain to a knowledge so sublime, Christ our Lord has taught us a manner of knowing Him more proportioned to our infirmity. For, He says, it is the property of sheep *to follow their shepherd, because they know his voice,* and to obey him; *But a stranger they follow not because they know not the voice of strangers.*[46] As if He would say: If thou desirest to be the sheep of Christ, thou must know thy supreme Pastor, fixing both thine eyes upon Him, that is, on His footsteps, that thou mayest follow Him,[47] considering the example He has left thee and the works He has done: attentive to His voice and least whisper, that thou mayest endeavour to know Him in the precepts and counsels of the law which He has promulgated; admiring the doctrine He preached, and obeying Him in all things, both commandments and inspirations; for this is to know Him perfectly as He Himself has told us: *I know Him and keep His word.*[48] If then thou knowest thy Pastor

---

[44] Cf. Rom 8:29
[45] Cf. Lk 9:28
[46] Jn 10:4, 14
[47] Cf. 1 Pt 2:21
[48] Jn 8:55

in this manner, He will brand thee with His own mark as His sheep, impressing the living image and likeness of Himself in the depth of thy soul; for He has said: *Whosoever shall do the will of My Father Who is in Heaven, he is My brother, and sister, and mother.*[49] He shall be His brother, for he shall receive from the eternal Father the image of His grace, by which he shall become like to Christ; he shall be also His mother, because he shall conceive Him spiritually within himself, forming within his soul a true image of Christ, as we have already said. Those who have attained to this loving knowledge of their Pastor, and are obedient to His behests, ought to glory therein more than in the knowledge of all other sciences or the possession of all earthly treasures.

This we learn from the words of God Himself, spoken by the mouth of Jeremias, *Let him that glorieth, glory in this, that he understandeth and knoweth Me;* knowing Me, He says, that he may form a true concept of Me; but understanding Me, that he may approve what he sees in Me: *For I am the Lord that exercise mercy, and judgement, and justice in the earth: for these things please Me,*[50] and they who know Me ought to do the same works as I do.

Beloved of my heart, from henceforth I desire to glory in that I know and love Thee as Thou desirest; making it all my delight to transform myself into the image of Thy beauty, passing from glory to glory, growing and increasing in Thy knowledge and love, until I see Thee in the brightness of Thy eternal glory. Amen.

---

[49] Mt 12:50
[50] Jer 9:24

Chapter III

That in the book of the life of Christ our Lord there are found seven things, in themselves very different, but here in a wonderful juxtaposition, which should be diligently meditated with due humility and charity.

AMONG THE WONDERS which God has worked, and still works daily in His elect, one of the most surprising, says St Bernard,[1] is that He has enabled the human mind to believe firmly truths very deep and sublime which can only be known by faith. For who would not be astonished to see an intellect, accustomed to follow its own light and to be guided by the senses, believe things which far surpass the grasp of the senses and human reason, still more when it believes them with as great certitude as if it saw them, felt them, and could understand them by natural light alone?

This is especially true of the mysteries of the life of Christ our Lord, in which are found things so great and at the same time so opposed to one another that they seem incompatible. Of these we may point out seven in particular which no one could understand unless the Saviour Himself had explained them to him and given him the faith necessary to believe them without hesitation. For ourselves, who do believe all that God has revealed, we ought to endeavour to perfect our faith by frequent and serious reflection on all these things, realising that there is no other way of acquiring a perfect knowledge of Christ our Lord, nor of admiring as we ought the wisdom, power

[1] St Bernard of Clairvaux, Sermon 3, on the *Vigil of the Nativity*

and charity which He has manifested in joining together for our salvation things in themselves so unlike and even contrary.

First. In the first place then, as being the source and root of all the rest, let us consider that He has united in one Person two different natures, the human and the divine; and this in such a way that although there is an infinite distance between God and man, between the life of a God and the life of a man, our Lord Christ is at once true God and true man; while He lived amongst us He lived at the same time a divine life and a human life, since He performed at the same time the actions proper to His Godhead, such as creating, preserving and governing the world, and the actions proper to man, such as eating, growing, feeling, reasoning, without the one either troubling or interrupting the other.

Second. Let us consider that His almighty power has joined together a blessed and glorious soul and a mortal and passible body, so that although one single man, He had two different kinds of life, the one in His soul, the other in His body. The first of these He had in common with the Blessed in highest Heaven, since His holy soul saw God face to face with immense joy and with all the advantages which those happy beings enjoy in Heaven. The second made Him like to men who are yet pilgrims on earth, *in via,* since His body was subject to those infirmities and miseries which we all have to suffer in this valley of tears. Even in His holy soul we find two things which could not exist together without a miracle, that is an extreme joy which He received from the clear vision of God and an extreme sorrow caused by the sight of our sins: these two things were joined together by the divine wisdom in order that this God-man, without detriment to that glory and majesty which belonged of right to a soul joined to the only-begotten Son of the eternal Father,² should at the same time have a *body fitted*³ to be immolated and to die for the salvation of the human race.

Third. From this proceeds the third union, namely that of a perfect man with an infant in the one Christ, who, while yet remaining in His mother's womb led the life of a perfect man as regards wisdom and discretion and the use of reason, as if He were already thirty years old, while at the same time He was leading the life of an infant in the same manner as all other infants do before the time of birth. During the whole time of His infancy he did nothing to distinguish Him from other infants, as though he were not already a perfect man. This is that *new thing* spoken of by the prophet Jeremias, that *a woman shall compass a man,*⁴ that is, should bear a man in her womb.

Fourth. To this we may add another union, utterly unknown before, that is of a child who has a mother but no father; a mother who yet remains a virgin. This was that stupendous *sign* given by Isaias to King Achaz: *Behold,* he said, *a virgin shall conceive, and bear a son, and His name shall be called Emmanuel,* that is, God with us, who shall be truly God; and nevertheless, *he shall eat butter and honey,* like other children.⁵

Fifth. The fifth union, which has stupefied the world, is the joining together of the highest glory with the deepest ignominy throughout the whole course of His life, from His nativity at Bethlehem to His death on Calvary, so that while He was leading a life of sublimest glory, as became the Son of God, in wisdom, sanctity and power (for He showed forth these three qualities in His wonderful works), at the same time He was leading a life utterly poor, hidden, laborious and contemptible. In the opinion of many, even His own near relatives, He passed

---

² Cf. Jn 1:4
³ Heb 10:5
⁴ Jer 31:22
⁵ Is 7:14-15

for an ignorant man, a fool, and even for a madman, although He was infinite wisdom; for a rogue, an enemy of God and a blasphemer, though He was sanctity itself; for a magician and one who worked pretended miracles, although He was the master of all nature and the Father had put all power into His hands.

Sixth. Let us consider how He has found an admirable means of reconciling two things not less opposed than the preceding, death and victory, ignominious crucifixion and glorious triumph. For at the very time that the Jews, incited by the evil spirits and transported by fury, hatred and envy, put Him to death upon the cross, He vanquished death, sin and Hell: His title to royalty was even attached to the wood on which He died with such ignominy and suffering; from that time forward He began to reign with sovereign authority over all creatures: whilst His mangled body reposed in the grave His victorious soul descended to Limbo, and despite all the infernal powers, rescued from that gloomy abode an infinite number of glorious trophies.

Seventh. This leads us to the last of these seven miracles we are considering, when His most holy soul by its own power was reunited to His dead body, reposing in the tomb. It rose immortal and impassible, yet still retaining the scars of those wounds in hands and feet and side which He had received at His crucifixion, for these were to witness for all eternity to the truth of His former mortality and the shame He had endured on the cross. After this, by His own power He ascended into Heaven, penetrating to the very throne of God, where He sits at the right hand of the Father. So that He who as man was lower than the angels is placed above the seraphim and cherubim, by reason of His divinity and the glory which is His as Son of God.

I pass over here that other wonderful union of things in themselves utterly dissimilar which the same Lord works by His omnipotence and daily renews in the most holy Sacrament of the altar, of which I shall speak at length in another chapter.

I. Of the manner in which we should meditate on all these things

Here then we have seven marvellous things in the life of God made man, which, for the incredulous, are like a sealed book. St Paul says they were *to the Jews a stumbling-block, and unto the Gentiles foolishness, but unto them that are called, both Jews and Greeks,* an open book, in which is resplendent *Christ* Himself, *the power of God and the wisdom of God;*[6] for it is by these admirable operations that they know and venerate Him. Yet are they filled with amazement and great admiration, as we read in the prophet Habacuc, according to the Septuagint version: *Lord,* he says, *I have considered Thy works and was afraid* or *stupefied: Thou shalt be known between two animals*[7] which words, say St Augustine[8] and St Jerome,[9] may be referred to both extremities of the life of Christ our Lord, which may be taken as a rule by which to interpret what passed between them. His first entry into the world was His birth in the stable at Bethlehem; His departure thence was His death on Mount Calvary. As soon as He was born He was placed in a crib, between two animals, and there He received the homage of both Jews and Gentiles: the *shepherds,* as the first-fruits of the Jews, were the first to offer Him their worship:[10] the Magi, as the first-fruits of the Gentile world,[11] followed to adore. As their *King,* they offered Him *gold,* as *God, incense,* and as mortal man, *myrrh.* The sight of such humility and abjection in no way diminished the idea they had conceived of His great majesty.

[6] 1 Cor 1:23-24
[7] Hab 3:2 *(Septuagint)*
[8] *St Augustine, City of God,* ch. 33
[9] In Hab 3
[10] Lk 2:16
[11] Mt 2:11

And when this same Lord was dead, He was fastened to a cross between two thieves, worse than brute beasts: yet even here He was recognised by the *centurion* although a Gentile, and many of the people, who *returned striking their breasts,* and saying: *Indeed this was a just man,*[12] and: *Truly, this was the Son of God;*[13] and *one of those robbers who were hanged* knew Him and confessed Him to be the King of Paradise, saying: *Remember me when Thou shalt come into Thy kingdom.*[14]

Was not the prophet right, then, when he cried out: *Lord, I have heard Thy hearing and was afraid;*[15] I could not see without admiration a God so humbled as to be born between two animals, and die between two thieves; but I was no less surprised to see Him overwhelmed with honour amongst these humiliations. What astonished me most was that those things which ought to have caused Him to be misjudged and despised have only served to make Him honoured and known both by Jews and Gentiles, by the ignorant and the learned, by the just and sinners, even by those men who, although little better than brute beasts, being enlightened from on high, have adored Him as their Saviour and their God.

O the depths of the riches of the wisdom and of the knowledge of God![16] O immense greatness of the bounty and divine omnipotence! Who could have appeared clothed with glory amidst such ignominy but the Creator of Heaven? What is there more strange than the annihilation of the only Son of God, become man to save men! Who would not admire this uncreated Wisdom in a manger, between two animals, hidden under the form of an infant whose eyes are not yet opened to

[12] Cf. Lk 23:48-49
[13] Mk 15:39, Mt 27:54
[14] Cf. Lk 23:39, 42
[15] Hab 3:1
[16] Rom 11:33

the light of day, and who seems indeed deprived of all light and consciousness? Who would not be astounded to behold the King of all might, the Saint of saints, in the form of a criminal between two thieves, as if He were Himself the chief of thieves? Who would not be struck dumb at seeing the Almighty either wrapped in swaddling bands or nailed to a cross? My beloved Saviour, *I have considered Thy works and I was afraid,* and in the midst of these two animals I have known Thee, who Thou art; as one whose knowledge, power and will were able to join together things so sublime with other things so vile, that Thou mightest cure my pride, warm my tepidity and inflame my heart with the fire of Thy love. My Beloved, the more I see Thee humbled for love of me, the dearer Thou art to me:[17] in Thy abjections I acknowledge Thy excellences, and I will glorify Thee as much in the one as in the other, willingly placing myself between two animals and between two thieves, desiring to pass for one ignorant and a sinner, that from this experience I may learn what Thou hast done for me and may obtain those virtues which Thou hast prepared for me.

But that thou mayest attain to a yet deeper knowledge of the perfection of Christ our Lord, it is well to notice with Eusebius and Theophylact[18] that instead of these words: *Thou shalt be known between two animals,* the Septuagint reads: *Thou shalt be known between two lives.*[19] What is meant by these two lives if not that divine and eternal life which our Saviour has always had as God, and the human and temporal life which He received as man? For those who wish to acquire a perfect knowledge of all the mysteries of His life from His Incarnation to His death ought to consider well the two sorts of life which

---

[17] *Quanto pro me vilior, tanto mihi carior.* St Bernard of Clairvaux, *Sermon 1 on the Epiphany, 1*

[18] Theophylact, *Ob accentum diversum.* Lib. 6 *Demonst. Evang.,* c. 15

[19] *In medio duarum vitarum cognosceris*

He lived and whose functions He fulfilled, in order to compare them one with another. For by this means they will gain a clear knowledge of the wisdom, goodness and omnipotence of Him who was able and has willed to unite them in His own person, that He might give us a certain hope and a kind of pledge of two other lives, which we ourselves may lead, the one human, according to nature, the other divine, according to grace, which He has united and which He conserves by unity of spirit.

If they gaze upon Him, for example, in the womb of His mother, where He was conceived by the operation of the Holy Ghost, and if they reflect on the life He led in this dark and narrow prison, they should straightway lift their eyes to Heaven, and look upon Him in the immense bosom of His Father who has begotten Him from all eternity, where He lives the same life as His Father, a divine life which both Father and Son communicate to the Holy Spirit with an inconceivable joy and love. If they consider Him in the crib, between two animals, or on the cross, between two thieves, and if they are astonished to see Him reduced to a life so poor, so contemptible, so filled with labours and sufferings, they ought at the same time to rise in spirit to highest Heaven and to contemplate Him full of majesty in the midst of cherubim and seraphim, seated on a throne where He enjoys a blissful and eternal life abounding with every kind of blessing, pleasure and joy, which He unceasingly imparts to His creatures.

After this, let them compare these two manners of life, so opposed to each other, and from them they will realise the immense bounty of their great God who has deigned to become man, not for His own interest or driven by any necessity, but from the most pure charity, with the sole object of showing us how much He loves us, how great care He has for our salvation, and how much He desires to honour us by this alliance of His grandeur with our vileness. Then they will cry out with the prophet: O Life of the living, *I considered thy works and I was afraid.* I considered the works of Thy divinity, the creation of the world, Thy providence in governing, the terrible plagues with which Thou didst strike Egypt, the wonders Thou didst work for Thy people Israel in dividing the Red Sea, raining manna from Heaven, drawing water from the rock, and staying the sun in the midst of His course; from all these prodigies I have learnt what Thou art and what Thou canst do. But what astonishes me most and makes me see most clearly Thy admirable perfections is when I see that Thou hast been able and hast willed to join together in Thyself these two lives, the human and the divine; for it is especially in this work that most marvellously appear Thy wisdom, Thy omnipotence, Thy justice, Thy mercy and Thy charity. Would that I could resemble Thee in both these lives! Would that I could bear Thy image on my heart and on my arm! Would that my outer man might be modelled on Thy sacred humanity, *bearing in my body the marks*[20] of Thy body and Thy continual *mortification,* that Thy *life also might be manifested* in mine.[21] Let my interior man also live as Thou didst live Thy divine life, renewed in spirit day by day and occupied in knowing, loving and enjoying Thee, so that *my life may be hid with* Thee *in God,*[22] transformed into Thy Deity for all eternity. Amen.

In the same way should we compare the other different manners of life exercised by our Lord in each mystery, applying them to the subject upon which we are meditating. For example, to regard Him in the crib as an infant and at the same time a perfect man; in the garden, as one enjoying beatific vision and therefore full of joy, and yet a mortal man full of sorrow. And if we consider the whole of His earthly life,

[20] Cf. Gal 6:17
[21] Cf. 2 Cor 4:10
[22] Cf. Col 3:3

we may always distinguish in His works both the human and the divine: we notice that for the relief of others He worked wonderful miracles, and took upon Himself all that was most painful, without ever using His divine power for His own needs. It is well also to examine how He has exercised certain virtues, which may be called human virtues, which belong in no way to God, such as poverty by the renunciation of all things, humility in bearing contempt, patience in labours, meekness in persecutions, obedience to precepts, compassion and sympathy for the evils of others.

Lastly, we may consider how He exercised and joined together those two lives, the active and the contemplative, in the midst of which He may be known. For at His baptism in the River Jordan He laid the foundations of the active life by the exercises of penance, and in His transfiguration He manifested the excellence of the contemplative life by the exercise of prayer: in both these places the voice of His heavenly Father declared Him to be His natural Son; that we might understand that in the midst of both these lives we may find Him and know Him, and by loving Him may be transformed into His living image by participation in His grace and charity.

II. Of the reasons for which our Lord has united in His own Person things so contrary

Let us now see the reasons which have induced this mighty God to unite in His own Person many things so utterly opposed, and how He has been able to join and harmonise them together. We may reduce these reasons principally to two: *one* on the part of God Himself who desired to reveal to us, as says St Augustine,[23] that immense fire of charity which burnt in

[23] *St Augustine, De catechizandis rudibus,* ch. 4. St Thomas Aquinas,

His divine breast; the *other* on the part of man, that He might repair the infinite misery of his sin and unite him with Himself in the union of this same charity. For it is the property of love, says St Denis,[24] to draw the lover out of Himself that He may communicate Himself to the object of His love; and although God may be said to have gone out of Himself in creating the world, that He might communicate Himself to His creatures in a multitude of ways; yet all this seemed so little to His infinite charity that He despised it as nothing, until that same infinite fire impelled Him so to forsake Himself as to communicate His own being, uniting His divine nature to a human nature in the Person of His Son. This fire of love is especially resplendent in this, that He did not choose an angelic nature, but that of man, who was His enemy and betrayer; for He could not give a more striking proof of love than to confer so infinite a boon on His enemy in order to change him into His friend.

This was declared by God Himself when He showed Himself to the prophet Ezechiel in the *likeness* and *appearance of a man… as it were the resemblance of amber,* which is a mixture of gold and silver, *as the appearance of fire within it round about: from his loins upward, and from his loins downward I saw as it were the resemblance of fire shining round about. As the appearance of the rainbow when it is in a cloud on a rainy day.*[25] Who is this man, asks St Gregory,[26] if not Jesus Christ our Lord, who has allied in His own Person the gold of His divinity with the silver of His humanity, fashioning this unity in the fire of infinite charity and love with which He has loved us? The fire, as the same saint declares,[27] until the mystery of Christ's

---

Summa Theologiae, IIIa, Q. 1, art. 2

[24] *St Denis, De divinis nominibus,* cap. 4

[25] Cf. Ez 1:27-28

[26] See St Jerome., *ibid.,* et St Gregory, *Hom.* 1 et 8 in Ez

[27] *ut supra*

generation as a human being should be accomplished, was if shut up in the bosom of God, and concealed in the deepest recesses of high Heaven. There, communicating Himself to the Angels, He set them on fire with His love; yet was He scarcely known to the greater part of men save to some few in Judaea. For although under the Old Law God worked many wondrous things for His people, yet these were but as sparks of that immense fire which should begin to spread over the earth as soon as the mystery of the Incarnation was accomplished, thus fulfilling the sign of the rainbow, by which He had promised to reconcile Himself with mankind, justifying them by a very rain of graces, appeasing the wrath of His Father and drying up that flood of sins with which the world was deluged.

Moreover, in the man seen in vision by the prophet, the rainbow of fire sent forth its rays from the loins to the feet, to signify that all the labours and all the works of the God-man, from the moment of His conception to that of His death, have had no other purpose than to enlighten souls and reconcile them with their Creator. For what induced Him to enclose Himself in the womb of a virgin, to be born in the stable and to be placed between two animals, to be circumcised and carried into Egypt; what obliged Him to allow Himself to be apprehended, scourged and put to death between two thieves? All this was done by the fire of charity, the rainbow of reconciliation and the rain of heavenly graces which He brought with Him from Heaven; wherever we contemplate Him, whether in the manger or on the cross, everywhere He cries out to us: *I am come to cast fire on the earth: and what will I, but that it be kindled?*[28] I am come that I might reconcile and save the world, and what will I, but that it be saved? I bring with Me copious graces and virtues which I will pour upon the earth like rain: what will I, but that they be poured upon all? Most

[28] Lk 12:49

sweet Saviour, fulfil this Thy desire in me, that I also may fulfil Thine, which is none other than Thy own. For Thou *art made to me my wisdom, justice, sanctification and redemption:*[29] fulfil in me this that Thou art made to me, that by the same I may serve Thee faithfully. Rise up, my soul, like another Moses and say to thyself: *I will go and see this great sight, why the bush is not burnt.*[30] I desire to contemplate the union of this divine fire with the bush of our humanity; I long to feel the heat of the flames, the sharp points of the thorns, the tender affections of the heart of Jesus and the cruel sufferings of His innocent body. I will gaze attentively on Him who has loved me so greatly, who has endured such horrible torments for love of me; I will come near Him, that the fire with which He burns may enlighten, enkindle and purify me, that the thorns with which He is crowned may wound me also, and by wounding, heal me. Divine fire, join the bush of my humanity to Thine, which is of a like nature, that I may be also joined to Thee in grace by the union of charity. Amen.

III. *Of the affections which proceed from all these things*

It is in this spirit that we should draw near to meditate on the mysteries of the life of Christ our Lord, in order to draw therefrom feelings and affections conformable to the end He set before Himself in uniting the two natures in one Person, in taking upon Him two lives and in performing with all possible perfection and care the functions of both. Above all ought we to strive to unite ourselves with God and to conform our lives to that of Jesus Christ; to be set on fire with the same fire which consumed Him, to profit by so many means which He

[29] 1 Cor 1:30
[30] Cf. Ex 3:3

has given us of obtaining reconciliation with His heavenly Father; to waste none of the graces He offers nor have any other affections but His, to labour at acquiring the virtues He recommends; that is, loving Him as He loves us, humbling ourselves as He humbled Himself, enduring as He endured and obeying as He obeyed.

Let no one, moreover, be discouraged at seeing the infinite distance there is between himself and God; for it is quite easy for His omnipotence to unite and join together things very unlike; neither let him lose confidence when he finds himself cold and dull of heart: because in one moment this divine fire is able to melt his ice and convert it into ardent affection; neither let him be made fearful by his sins: for as God looks upon this heavenly rainbow, He will remember the compact He has made with him and will forgive him if he comes before Him with humble confession. If he finds himself in the presence of God as a dry land without water,[31] let him understand that Christ is like an immense cloud ready to rain down innumerable graces to water the dry ground of his heart and bring forth abundance of fruit. Lastly, if he accustom himself to meditate daily on the mysteries of the life of our Saviour, he will conceive fervent desires of imitating Him in the practice of all virtues and of advancing daily in the path of perfection.

This has been shown to us by the Spouse in the Canticle: *While the king was at his repose, my spikenard sent forth the odour thereof.*[32] Where is this chamber of His repose and the place where the King of Heaven is wont to make a banquet for His chosen guests, save the meditation of these mysteries?

What is the spikenard which gives forth its odour in the presence of the King except the virtues which are most pleas-

[31] Cf. Ps 62:3
[32] Cant 2:11

ing in His sight? For spikenard, says St Gregory[33] and St Bernard,[34] is a certain small plant, of a hot nature, very warming to the breast. It gives out also a strong perfume, especially when bruised. It may therefore be taken to represent humility, which flies from exaltation, and charity, which inflames the heart; penitence also and contrition, which blot out sin, and fervour of spirit, which repels torpor; and lastly, devoutness of soul, which gives forth sweet-smelling affections and exemplary works.

All these virtues give out their odour, that is produce their acts, while the King is in the place of His repose; for in whatever place we fix our eyes upon Him, we should immediately annihilate ourselves in the abyss of our nothingness, either on account of the humiliation which our sins deserve, or for the rare example of humility given by the King Himself. And why should not a slave humiliate himself when he sees his King so humbled; for it would be intolerable impudence, says St Bernard,[35] for a vile little worm of earth to be proud, seeing how the divine majesty has humbled Itself; God humbles Himself to cure man's pride, and shall not man humble himself in imitation of God's humility? And if the sight of thy own misery is not enough to humble thee, what of the infinite charity of thy Saviour, humiliating Himself to repair thy pride? Supreme King, seeing myself thus humbled in Thy presence, *my spikenard will give forth its odour;* yet this odour is not mine but Thine, and is moreover produced by Thy virtue and example and in imitation of the odour of Thy humility, which Thy spikenard gives forth with so much more excellence than mine, since it is a so much greater thing for the Creator to abase Himself than for a creature to humble himself however much. But, Lord, I would join my spikenard to Thine, my humility to

---

[33] St Greory., *ibid*
[34] St Bernard of Clairvaux, Sermon 42 on the *Canticle of Canticles*
[35] Sermon 1 on the Nativity

Thine, that the perfume of both being mingled together, it may ascend as a sweet-smelling odour in the nostrils of our heavenly Father, so that for Thy sake, in whom He is ever well-pleased, I also may be found worthy to find favour in His sight.

In the presence of this supreme King the spikenard of charity will give out its own perfume, namely, most loving and tender affections like to those of the King Himself, and suited to the dispositions of those who contemplate Him. So, if their sins trouble them, it will bring forth affections of loving contrition when it sees how displeasing they are to our Lord, and all that He has done and suffered to heal them. With Magdalen, they will feel impelled to prostrate themselves at His feet, that they may *anoint* them with the *ointment* of this spikenard,[36] sorrowfully uniting their affections with His and imploring Him to pardon and heal their sins. But if they rejoice in the hope that their transgressions are already forgiven, then their spikenard will exhale affections of gratitude and praise; still keeping company with Magdalen, they will conceive the desire of *anointing His head*,[37] uniting fervent aspirations after the highest perfection with those actions of great worth which He performed: that as members of His mystical body they may be joined to their Head and receive an influx of that eternal life which He came to give. And how should not this spikenard, which is nothing else than the most perfect charity, burn and give forth its best odours when it is brought near to that glowing fire which inflames the very heart of God Himself?

O man, says St Augustine,[38] *if you are slow to make offers of love, at least be not slow in returning love* to Him who has so greatly loved you; love Him who has first loved you, who at

---

[36] Cf. Lk 7:38, Jn 12:3
[37] Cf. Mt 26:7, Mk 14:3
[38] *Si amare pigebat, salterm redamare non pigebat.* St Augustine, *De catechizandis rudibus*, ch. 4

every hour presents you with ever fresh proffers of love; who in return for His own infinite love only asks a love as limited as yours. Infinite Lover, I long to love Thee as Thou lovest me, so that thus I may satisfy my desire of loving: but I would unite and join my love with Thine, that Thine may inflame and perfect mine; would that I might be so drawn into and dissolved in myself that I might be wholly lost in Thee and produce fragrant perfumes of very fervent love. Amen.

In the same manner we may put in practice the other virtues, being careful to accommodate their acts and exercises to our own state and dispositions, exhaling our own odour, not that of others. For in the sight of the supreme King the spikenard of novices and of the perfect, of superiors and their subjects, or of the religious of different Orders ought to produce the fragrance proper to the state of each. Perhaps this is why the Apostle said: *Put ye on the Lord Jesus Christ*;[39] signifying that as our garments should be made to fit us, neither too wide nor too strait, nor overlong: so also should we put on the virtues, works and affections of Jesus Christ according to our capacity and our present need. Yet our desires may be without limit and extend even to all that our Saviour did and suffered: but the resolutions which we intend straightway to put in practice ought to be suited to our state and proportioned to our present strength.

When therefore we are about to begin our prayer, let us think that we are about to put on Jesus Christ and make ourselves as like Him as we can in the mystery upon which we are about to meditate. In order to accomplish this we have four things to do: the first is to recall to mind how much He has loved us; next, we must listen to the words He will speak to our heart; let us consider, moreover, all that He has done for us; lastly, let us try to realise something of what He has suffered.

[39] Rom 13:14, Gal 3:27

By thus clothing ourselves with His likeness we may come to love Him in some degree as He has loved us, to obey His orders, and to offer ourselves to imitate Him in those things He has done and suffered: yet all this in that degree and perfection which shall be granted us and in the manner we are about to explain in the succeeding chapters.

Chapter IV

Of the knowledge of Christ our Lord in those things which He did on His first entry into this world... that is, in the mysteries of His Incarnation and His Nativity.

AS THERE ARE many things to be read and meditated on during the whole course of the life of Christ our Lord, of which we have spoken at length in the book of *Meditations*, we will only add here some considerations concerning the beginning and end of this divine book, by which we may easily judge of what is written between.

For it is clear that the virtues of our Lord shone forth with special brilliance both at His entry into this world and His leaving it. From the very first He desired to teach us how to begin a life which should be all spiritual and to lay early the foundations of true perfection, according to that saying: *Well begun is half done.* Those therefore who desire to enter either into the bosom of Holy Church or into the religious state, or to change their whole conduct, should begin their new life as the Son of God began His: since, according to St Cyprian,[1] the beginning of the life of the Son of God ought to serve us as a model for the beginning of our spiritual life. But it is chiefly in His departure from this world that He has revealed Himself, because *He loved His own... unto the end*,[2] showing them much greater proofs of love at the end than He had done at the beginning: that they might learn to imitate Him in this

---
[1] St Cyprian, *Sermon on the Nativity*
[2] Jn 13:1

also, growing day by day in sanctity the more rapidly as they approach their end, humbly imploring God, as David says,[3] to guard with special care their *coming in and going out,* and thus to secure their full perfection.

The advent of Christ our Lord into the world may be considered under two aspects, the one hidden in His incarnation and conception, when He took the nature of man by entering into the womb of a Virgin; the other open and manifest in His nativity, when He was born into this world in the cave at Bethlehem and *was seen upon earth and conversed with men.*[4] The first of these represented the contemplative or unitive life, which is wholly interior and recollected; in the second He gave us an example of the active life which is occupied in exterior works for the good of our neighbour. Yet these two lives were never separated in Christ our Lord, who in both has left us admirable examples of heroic virtue.

I. Of four virtues exercised by Christ our Lord in the womb of His blessed Mother

From the first moment of His entrance into the world our Lord united the functions of a perfect man to the body of a little infant, in which state He exercised three most excellent virtues which are commemorated by the prophet Jeremias, saying: *It is good for a man when he hath borne the yoke from his youth. He shall sit solitary and hold his peace: because he hath taken it up upon himself.*[5] Who is it that deserves the name of Man by excellence except Christ our Saviour, who elected to become man and to pass through the various ages of human

[3] Ps 120:8
[4] Cf. Bar 3:38
[5] Lam 3:27, 28

existence, like other men, that He might join together the feebleness of an infant with the virtues of a perfect man? In a stupendous and hitherto unheard of manner He began, from the first moment of His conception, to be a man and to bear the yoke of the Lord: *sitting* for nine months in the womb of a woman, *holding His peace* in utter *solitude,* and *raising Himself* in immense majesty *above Himself:* that by His example He might teach us how best to enter upon life at the first dawning of reason; if it is already too late for us to do this, let us now at least endeavour to make a fresh start, at whatever age we may have arrived.

In the first place, at the moment of His Incarnation, He offered himself generously to *bear the yoke* of perfect obedience, and subjection to the will of His eternal Father, His holy laws and all that He had decreed concerning Him. This had been beautifully brought out by the Apostle, commenting on the words which were spoken by David in the Person of the Saviour, saying: *When He cometh into the world He saith* to His eternal Father: *Behold I come: in the head of the book it is written of Me: that I should do Thy will, O God;* yes, my God, I am resolved to do it and I have placed *Thy law in the midst of My heart.*[6] From the first moment of His existence this most holy Saviour knew all that was foretold of Him in the Holy Scriptures; all that He was to do and suffer, and especially what the eternal Father had written concerning Him in His book of eternal predestination, on whose first page it was set down that He was to be the head and chief of the predestinate. And although it was predicted that He should suffer innumerable pains, torments and insults, He embraced them all with unspeakable joy and love, placing them in the midst of His heart as things most precious and dear to Him, offering Himself to fulfil them without omitting one jot or tittle. O how wonderful

[6] Cf. Heb 10:5-7, Ps 39:7-9

was the obedience, how perfect the resignation and burning the charity which produced this obedience so swiftly that not for one moment would He defer His acceptance, nor leave one single point unfulfilled; He placed them in the midst of His heart with such joy and perseverance that never did He slacken or fail in anything: so that when He had reached the last moment of His life, finding one thing yet remaining to be accomplished *that the Scripture* might be fulfilled, He said: *I thirst, and when He had taken the vinegar* which was offered to Him, said*: It is consummated*[7] and fulfilled, whatever was written of Me in my Father's book, and I have accomplished all that I offered Myself to do at the moment of My Incarnation. Thanks be to Thee, most sweet Saviour, for that generous will with which Thou didst offer Thyself to bear so heavy a yoke; grant me from henceforth to subject my will to Thine and to *take up Thy yoke* with such love that I may reckon it *light,* just because it is Thine.[8] Learn, O my soul, to read along with thy Saviour whatever is written concerning thee in the book of His law, for it is written in order that thou shouldst carry it out; say to Him with a resolute and courageous heart: *Behold I come,* ready to accomplish whatever Thou shalt command; Thy will shall be mine and it shall be ever whole and entire *in the midst of my heart.*

Secondly, as soon as this oblation was made, our Saviour embraced that solitude and silence which He had chosen for His portion on His first entrance into the world. Although He could have assumed the body of a full-grown man, as He had created Adam in Paradise, yet He willed to begin His life in the condition and age of an infant, compelling Himself to undergo the solitude, silence and confinement of His mother's womb. In this prison He dwelt, practising a kind of general mortifi-

[7] Jn 19:28, 30
[8] Cf. Mt 11:30

cation of all those things which in this world serve to recreate and delight the senses: from that moment beginning to offer the sacrifice of Himself joined to a voluntary abnegation of all the delectable and visible things of this life. And although other infants do not suffer this, since they have not the use of reason nor know even in what place they are, yet this most blessed child, in that He was perfect man, knew and was conscious of all His surroundings. By this example He would teach those who must needs appear in public and converse with their fellow-men, how necessary it is for them from time to time to go apart and converse in secret and silence with God; for this end also, later on, He retired into the desert, remaining there forty days before coming forth to begin His public ministry.

But since solitude and silence of body profit little unless they are joined to solitude and silence of spirit, this He also embraced at the same moment with still greater goodwill. For solitude of spirit is to be free from all images, thoughts of and affections to creatures, which, by occupying and disturbing the heart, hinder intercourse and union with God. But silence of the spirit consists in this, that a man no longer occupies himself with creatures nor speaks with them interiorly but with God alone: in this holy solitude and silence Christ our Lord always dwelt, even when in the company of others: for He said of Himself that although He came down from Heaven, yet He was always in Heaven;[9] for the Heaven where He dwelt was His own blessed soul, ever occupied with God and heavenly things.

At this same time He began to *raise Himself above Himself*[10] by the sublime exercises of prayer and contemplation. For at the same moment that He saw Himself raised to the infinite dignity of Son of God by the hypostatic union, He raised Himself also above the Cherubim and Seraphim to perfect

[9] Cf. Jn 3:13
[10] Lam 3:28, *quia levavit super se* (Vulgate)

union with God by knowledge, love and fruition: at that same moment He beheld also the divine essence, in which, as in a most glorious book, He read all things past, present and to come for all eternity. And beholding that infinite bounty He embraced it with the arms of charity and with intensest love, exulting in the possession of such immense joy. From His heart poured forth all the affections that prayer can produce, now praising and glorifying God for the infinite excellences He saw in Him, now returning immense gratitude and thanks for the innumerable benefits He had received, now adoring, and imploring His heavenly Father to make His glory known throughout the whole world and impetrating fresh favours for mankind, now become His brethren. In this manner He began that prayer which continued without cessation throughout the whole course of His mortal life, *with a strong cry and tears,* as says the Apostle,[11] converting His Mother's womb into an oratory very differently than did Jonas the belly of the whale.[12]

Most sweet Saviour, who in Thy Mother's womb didst ascend *the mountain of myrrh* and *the hill of frankincense*[13] uniting this sublime mortification to prayer yet more sublime, teach me to build in my own soul a house of solitude wherein I may be silent and pray in secret, and by raising myself above myself, may become one with Thee for all eternity. Amen.

To these three virtues our Lord added a fourth, which is their fruit, that is an ardent zeal for the salvation of souls, which from that instant began to devour His entrails and which impelled Him to come to the assistance of His brethren by the prayers and oblations which He offered on their behalf. Inflamed with this divine fire, He omitted nothing which could

[11] Heb 5:7
[12] Cf. Jonas 2:2
[13] Cant 4:6

promote this divine office of Saviour. First He communicated to His holy Mother an infinite number of gifts and graces; by her means He sanctified His holy Precursor St John, filling Him with the Holy Spirit and with many notable graces. From this He would have contemplatives learn that while they raise themselves above themselves by intimate communion with God, they still should not neglect their neighbours; on the contrary, they should go out of themselves and abandon the care of their own affairs to help their brethren in need, either by their own prayers and penances, or by means of others, to whom this talent has been committed: they themselves assisting by their zeal and their prayers, as we shall explain further on.

As to ourselves, if we would ascend to the summit of the contemplative life, we must imitate our Lord in these four virtues, enclosing ourselves in the bosom of God, there to live separated from the world and closely united with Him who will take in our regard the place not only of father, but also mother, since in the words of the prophet, we are *carried by His bowels and borne up by His womb*,[14] as long as this life shall last. Enter then into the Divinity, which will surround thee on every side, as the child is enclosed in his mother's womb, and, there, *hidden with Christ*,[15] pray along with Him, taking Him as thy Master and as thy helper and model in prayer.

My heavenly Master, who didst *spend the whole night in the prayer of God*,[16] and at Thy first coming into the world didst spend nine months of darkness in Thy Mother's womb in most sublime prayer: teach me to pray the prayer of God, by which I may enter into God Himself and there converse with Him apart, so that no creature soever may hinder me.

[14] Is 46:3
[15] Cf. Col 3:3
[16] Cf. Lk 6:12

II. Of four other virtues which Christ our Lord exercised at the time of His Nativity

When our Lord was first seen in the world in visible form, that is at His birth in the cave at Bethlehem, He displayed an admirable fervour of spirit, as if laying the foundations of all evangelical perfection. On which account the Scripture said of Him: *God will come from the south, and the Holy One from Mount Pharan;*[17] for, as St Gregory explains it,[18] God is said to come from that place where He is manifested: Christ our Lord was manifested in Bethlehem, which is to the south of Jerusalem; thence He came, there He was born of a Virgin-mother, by the operation of the Holy Spirit. This Virgin, signified by Mount Pharan, or the *shady mountain,* being overshadowed by the Holy Spirit, brought forth her Son, yet without detriment to her virginity. And in this same place the Saviour first manifested Himself by works of most admirable fervour, like the light and heat of the noonday sun streaming through a cloud, with no less light than heat. For being filled with the Holy Spirit, He practised virtues outwardly indeed insignificant and obscure, yet in themselves admirable and truly worthy of Him.

The matter of these was provided by four things equally painful and humiliating, yet which He embraced with all affection without in any way derogating from His majesty and grandeur: these were poverty, contempt, suffering and labour. Some of these came upon Him from His enemies, others He Himself elected to undergo for the help and assistance of His brethren, yet always by His own free choice and acceptance. They had also been foretold by the prophet David, speaking in the Person of the Saviour, saying: *I am poor and in labours from*

---

[17] Hab 3:3, according to the Septuagint: *De monte umbroso et condenso*
[18] St Gregory the Great, Moralia in Job, B.31, ch. 18

my youth; and being exalted have been humbled and troubled.[19] He did indeed begin to undergo these labours from His youth, even from the very day of His nativity: on these four things of which we have spoken, as on a most solid foundation, He erected four virtues which are like the four supporting columns of all evangelical perfection.

For in the first place He exercised heroic POVERTY OF SPIRIT, even to the deprivation of all earthly possessions. When He was about to be born, He forsook His home and all the commodities He might have enjoyed at Nazareth to betake Himself to Bethlehem where He was forced to beg hospitality as a mendicant. This being denied Him in the city, He chose the vilest and most abject of places in which to be born, namely a stable, where a manger was His only cradle.

To poverty He joined her sister HUMILITY OF HEART, choosing for His portion contempt and abasement; not content with the lowest and most despised place of birth and to be laid on straw between two animals, He added this also, on the eighth day to be circumcised, that is to bear in His innocent body the character of a sinner. For His love could not be satisfied with clothing Himself in our human nature; it induced Him also to take upon Himself the mark of our fallen state. In this lowly condition He was glorified by the Angels and adored by the Magi: yet the honour they paid Him was soon followed by yet greater humiliation and contempt.

To these two sisters He added a third, heroic PATIENCE in sufferings. These He began to taste of without delay, both from the inclemency of the weather, choosing to be born in mid-winter that He might experience the severity of intense cold; or from the sharp knife of circumcision which cut His delicate flesh and caused Him to shed the first precious drops of that blood which was to be the ransom of mankind. But

[19] Ps 87:16

a few days later He was driven from Bethlehem by the cruel persecution of Herod and forced to fly through desert places to Egypt, where His sufferings would be still more severe.

The fourth virtue which He added to these three was, I say, a certain immense FERVOUR OF SPIRIT caused by the ardour of His charity and His zeal for His Father's glory and the salvation of souls. However great His sufferings, He received them all with the greatest joy for our consolation and example, and as a remedy for all our ills. He desires also that we should take them for the chief subject of our meditation, so that, imitating His patience, we may say with the Spouse: *A bundle of myrrh is my Beloved to me, He shall abide between my breasts.*[20]

Consider then, my soul, how like thy Beloved is to this tree which of itself distils myrrh from all its pores, but when its bark is cut or injured, gives forth greater abundance. For His whole life was one continual exercise of poverty, contempt, suffering and labour; some of these subjects of mortification He underwent of His own free choice, others came from His enemies, who pierced Him with a thousand wounds and cruelly ill-treated Him in His Person, His honour and even His very life. Approach then to this mysterious tree, consider attentively the sufferings of thy Saviour; strive to imprint at least some of them in thy memory, that thou mayest meditate on them at leisure. Make of them for thyself a bundle of myrrh, and remember what St Bernard says,[21] that it is not upon thy shoulders but upon thy breast that thou shouldst carry it, in order to have it ever before thine eyes, and gaze on it with complaisance and love, since the sight of an object so moving will win thy heart and there produce two movements of affection, one of compassion, the other of gratitude. For it is impossible to see what Jesus has suffered for us without being deeply touched and returning Him infinite thanks.

[20] Cant 1:12
[21] St Bernard of Clairvaux, Sermon 45 *on the Canticle of Canticles*

Do not content thyself with looking only, but make, according to the counsel of St Gregory,[22] another little bundle of various acts of mortification and of those four virtues which thou hast seen the Son of God practise with such excellence; desire with thy whole heart to imitate Him in His nakedness, contempt, labours and sufferings: so that thou mayest find occasion to follow Him also in the exercise of poverty and humility, patience and fervent zeal, binding together this little bundle with affections of charity and love, *which is the bond of perfection.*[23] So it will come about that however much myrrh thou gatherest, thou wilt never need to complain of having too much, and scarcely wilt thou find enough to make a very small bundle, because love will render light a burden which of itself would overwhelm thee, and will convert into spiritual delight all the mortifications of the flesh. And indeed, how couldst thou not find that a light bundle which God Himself has suffered for thee, becoming a little infant for thy sake? How shouldst thou not place it on thy breast, when He has carried it on His own? How shouldst thou condemn to oblivion and bear on thy back that which He has kept ever before His eyes? Neither do thou make up thy bundle of one kind of virtue only, but unite them all together: for one alone will be heavy, but united, they will weigh light. For humility makes poverty sweet, patience is joyful when joined with charity, and charity itself makes even humility lovable. For what is difficult in one virtue is surmounted by the help of another, and there is not one which does not seem easy when practised in the company of Him who possesses them all in a sovereign degree.

Beloved of my heart, from henceforth Thou shalt be to me a little bundle of fragrant myrrh; I will so love Thee that whatever I see in Thee shall be to me sweet and joyful; the odour of Thy

[22] *In Cant*
[23] Col 3:14

myrrh, just because Thou hast carried it, shall comfort and strengthen me, and shall be my continual delight. I will love Thee as Thou hast loved me: so shall it become sweet to me to suffer for Thee whatever Thou hast borne for me.

Let us now proceed to the consideration of those things which our same Lord forsook and renounced in order to take upon Himself the four penalties of which we have spoken above. We may with profit keep this thought before our minds: Our great Redeemer might have willed to make His entry into the world adorned in a manner worthy of His state and dignity, for in strict justice He should have possessed the four splendid endowments proper to glorified bodies; that is brightness, impassibility, subtility and agility. But because He desired a body fitted to be immolated for us,[24] He freely renounced these advantages and took upon Himself all that could be found most shameful, hard and painful in this life. In place of the gift of brightness He clothed himself with ignominy, for impassibility He took suffering, for subtility the burden of poverty, and for agility, labours and weariness. It was in garments such as these that He first came into the world, putting aside the precious vestment till He should return to take possession of the kingdom of His Father. It is true that on Mount Thabor He appeared, His face shining like the sun;[25] but this glory quickly passed and He immediately took off this splendid garment which He had only put on as if to try it and to animate His flesh to suffer by the hope of the perfect beatitude which was prepared for Him in Heaven. Then He at once descended the mountain, His mind bent on the journey to *Jerusalem* where He was to *accomplish the death*[26] of which He had *spoken with*

---

[24] Cf. Heb 10:5, Ps 39:7-9
[25] Cf. Mt 17:2
[26] Vulg., *excessus*, literally *decease*

Moses and Elias,[27] clothed now in that garment of mortality which consisted in poverty, contempt, sufferings and labours, which His great charity impelled Him to put on. For in enduring all these things our most sweet Jesus desired to *exceed* and, if it be lawful to say so, to overpass all measure: doing and suffering for us much more than was actually necessary for our redemption, His immense love seeming to carry Him out of Himself, so that He cared not to what *excess* He went.

Fix thy eyes therefore upon this true Joseph in His *coat of many colours*[28] descending to His feet, which the eternal Father had made for His Son, woven from the aforesaid four penalties, dyed in His own blood by the envy of His brethren. But notice that though He put it on as an infant, and that it then fitted His tiny stature, nevertheless, as He grew in age, the garment grew also with Him, proportioning itself to His strength until at length He succumbed to its weight. For throughout His whole life His poverty was extreme, He *had not where to lay His head,*[29] *He was filled with reproaches*[30] He was the *Man of Sorrows*[31] wearied with many labours. As long as He lived He bore this heavy yoke; He carried His cross continually, drinking His most bitter *chalice* and *baptised* with a terrible *baptism.*[32] But in the hour of death He surpassed Himself, redoubling His sufferings and multiplying His sorrows, that He might in some measure satisfy His extreme love, which, after all the labours of His life was not yet fully content: lastly He shed His very blood, and being both high priest and victim, He offered himself willingly in expiation for our offences.

[27] Cf. Lk 9:31
[28] Gen 37:3
[29] Lk 9:58
[30] Lam 3:30
[31] Is 58:3
[32] Cf. Mk 10:38

Let us humbly enquire the reason why He put on this garment at His nativity, continuing to wear it throughout His life and even dying in it. We may hear Him answer that He did this to confound the children of this world who clothe themselves with the garment of the *old man*[33] woven from four of the glories of this world: these are riches, honours, pleasures and comforts; from which proceed cupidity, pride, fleshly desires and idleness, the enemies of eternal salvation.

Supreme Master, from this moment I cast off that garment of the *old man* which thou didst so abhor, but I will *put on the new man* and his virtues which Thou hast so loved. I will prefer Thy poverty to all the treasures of the world; I will make more account of Thy ignominy than of all the world's honours and dignities; I will esteem Thy sorrows and labours above every perishing delight and solace. Reserve the garment and the gifts of glory for my portion in the next life: for me, during my earthly pilgrimage it shall be glory enough to be clothed as Thou wert.

Such is the principal fruit we ought to draw from these considerations. Let us be persuaded that in order to obtain the blessing of our heavenly Father we must imitate Jacob,[34] stripping ourselves of our ordinary clothing in which we resemble the earthly Adam to put on the precious garments of Christ Jesus our Brother, embracing all the sufferings of our mortal life in union with His. And then the odour of this garment will incite the eternal Father to fill us with blessings both in this life and the next. In exchange for poverty He will give us the riches of His grace; for insults He will show us great favour; for sufferings He will fill us with consolation, and for labour with joy ineffable.

Let us remember that the soldiers who crucified Christ *divided His garments*[35] into four parts, that a part might fall

[33] Cf. Col 3:9, 10
[34] Cf. Gen 27:15
[35] Mt 27:35, Jn 19:23

to each of them; but instead of dividing His *coat* which *was without seam woven from the top throughout* they *cast lots for it.* From this we learn that when Christ our Lord distributes His goods to His heirs, who are His soldiers, He divides between them His robe which is composed of four pieces: to some He gives poverty; to others humiliations; to some He sends sorrow and sickness; on others He lays labours and fatigue in the exercise of their office or ministry. But the most fortunate are those for whom He keeps the coat without seam, that coat which cannot be divided because it is woven throughout from the top to the bottom; such are those whom He tries in every kind of way from the beginning of their life until the end; these He replenishes with such consolations in the midst of the greatest bitterness that they find nothing too hard to undertake for the sake of Him who has suffered all for them. Blessed indeed are those whom He thus favours, to whom we may apply those words of the Psalmist: *The lines are fallen unto me in goodly places.*[36] For although they may seem despicable in the eyes of the world, they are most noble and precious in the sight of Christ; for He has clothed them with Himself.

Most dear Redeemer, in whose hands my lot lies, I desire nothing better than to imitate the sufferings Thou hast endured and the virtues Thou hast exercised in them; for I am sure that if I have on this *garment,* Thou wilt not exclude me from the *marriage feast,*[37] but being admitted to it, I shall reign and rejoice with Thee for all eternity. Amen.

---

[36] Ps 15:6
[37] Cf. Mt 22:11

Chapter V

Of the reading and meditation of the book of Jesus Christ crucified.... Eight excellent properties of the unitive love which shines forth from the Cross.

THE SHORTEST AND MOST EFFICACIOUS means of learning the science of the spirit is the study of Jesus crucified, stretched out upon the cross like an open book wherein all who have eyes may study and understand the secrets of the spiritual life. This is clearly taught by the great Apostle who, although rapt into the third heaven and shown there ineffable mysteries, yet told his disciples that he *judged not* himself *to know anything among* them *but Jesus Christ and Him crucified.*[1] He meant them to understand that these great mysteries which had been revealed to him were all comprised in Jesus crucified, that it sufficed to know Jesus crucified to possess all that goes to make up true and perfect wisdom, and that the sole subject of his meditations, discourses, and letters was Jesus crucified. It is indeed the only book which we should have at all times before our eyes; the doctrine which it contains is that on which we ought to meditate, which we ought to preach, which should be our necessary rule of life and conduct.

Let us then take up this book, and according to the saying of Job, *carry it upon* our *shoulder and put it about* us *as a crown. At every step,* He says, *I would pronounce it, and offer it as to a prince,*[2] namely, the King of Heaven, as the best of all reasons

[1] 1 Cor 2:2
[2] Job 31:36, 37

why He should pour upon us His grace and mercy. No one can excuse himself from reading it; for, as says the blessed Laurence Justinian,[3] it is made alike for the ignorant and the learned, for worldly people as well as for the spiritual; all will find in it whatever is most suitable to their condition. As it is a *book written within and without*,[4] and the simple will read only the exterior, whereon appears nothing but shame and suffering; the more enlightened will penetrate deeper and will find extraordinary graces and virtues. What is written without is inscribed by the hand of executioners, who use no other pen than scourges, thorns and nails; what is written within is from the finger of God, who made use of the powers of that most holy soul to form acts of the most heroic virtues. The prophet Ezechiel, who had read and considered this book, notices in it principally three things, *lamentations and canticles and woe:*[5] in truth it is full of powerful incentives to weep over our sins, to give thanks to God for His benefits, or to dread the chastisements with which His justice threatens us.

I. How we may best profit by these three motives in our meditations on the Passion

First then let us read the *lamentations* of this book, all that is sorrowful and mournful; we must make serious reflections on the sufferings both interior and exterior with which the Son of God was overwhelmed in soul and body: the sight of so many torments undergone by this divine Lamb, who came to wash out the sins of mankind, will excite us to weep for our own.

[3] *De triumph. agon. Christi,* cap. 10
[4] Apoc 5:1, Ez 2:9
[5] Ez 2:9

Let us enter in spirit into the garden and see how He Himself causes the beginning of His passion: He sets before Himself in one view all the ignominy and all the pain which is being prepared for Him, and He sets them before Himself so vividly that He is seized with fear, sadness, sorrow and distress; He falls into a mortal agony and His soul, filled with the terrifying notion of so much shame and suffering, already feels all that He will have to endure up to His last breath. And that we may know what He is suffering in the depths of His soul, He lets it be seen in a sweat of blood which exudes from all the pores of His body, and clearly indicates the excess of His affliction. If the mere thought of the chains, scourges, thorns and nails so afflicts Him that He sheds, as it were, tears of blood, what will it be when these chains closely bind His arms, when these scourges lacerate His shoulders, when these thorns pierce His brow, when these nails transfix His hands and feet? Sinner, what ought to be your feelings at the sight of such a spectacle? How can you read the lamentations of this book without floods of tears pouring from your own eyes, weeping with Him who weeps, because you are the principal cause of His weeping?

But in order that you may feel more deeply the excess of His pains, picture to yourself that He reproaches you with the greatness and multitude of your crimes, which can only be expiated by such horrible torments: detest, then, your ingratitude and admire the charity of your Saviour, who has indeed willed to be punished in your place and to make full satisfaction to the divine justice by sorrows and humiliation as yet unheard of. But while you think on the pains which He has suffered for crimes of which He was innocent, remind yourself of those to which you ought voluntarily to submit for the faults of which you are really guilty. Let these cruel *thorns* penetrating His head teach you how detestable are pride and ambition: let the *gall* and *vinegar* which were given Him to drink show you how you ought to mortify your taste and overcome intemperance: this shameful *nakedness* which He endures upon the cross points out the path of general renunciation of everything worldly: the *nails* which pierce His hands and feet may serve to show you how you ought to crucify your flesh with its passions and disorderly desires: His *heart,* opened by the spear, should make you see how you ought to open your heart both to God to receive His holy inspirations and to the priest to confess your sins: this *blood* which flows from all His veins will warn you to resist sin even to the shedding of your own, if need be, sooner than consent to the least fault. Lastly, the drastic nature of the remedy ought to show you how perilous was your condition, as St Bernard tells us.[6] Realise, then, what sort of wounds they are which could only be healed by those of your Saviour; unless they had been unto death and indeed eternal, the Son of God would never have endured so cruel a death to provide a remedy.

If all these considerations are not sufficient to soften your heart, at least fear the calamities with which God threatens you. Read in this book of the Crucified the *menaces* and *woes* written in it; for all these wounds of Jesus are so many characters signifying the horror of the punishments which God has prepared for those who persist in sin, as our Lord Himself said to the daughters of Jerusalem: *For if in the green wood they do these things, what shall be done in the dry?*[7] If a tree still green and fit to bear fruit is torn up before its time, will the dry and barren tree be spared? All these temporal pains which I suffer for the sins of others represent the eternal pains which the criminals themselves ought to suffer for their own sins; in My *thorns* they may consider the cruel remorse which will for ever pierce their conscience; in My *thirst,* that raging thirst with

[6] St Bernard of Clairvaux, Sermon 1 *On the Nativity*
[7] Lk 23:31

which they will burn without ever obtaining, any more than Dives, a single drop of water to slake it; in My *nakedness* the confusion in which they will eternally be plunged; in My *nails,* the fetters with which their hands and feet will be loaded, so that they can never perform any good work nor escape from their prison; in the *wound* of My *side,* that worm which will perpetually devour their conscience; in My *sadness, agony* and *desertion,* their sadness, their agonies, the extreme state of abandonment in which they are and will be for all eternity, ever miserable and ever inconsolable because they have despised and trodden under foot the blood which I have poured out for their salvation, that blood which is the ink with which I shall write the sentence of their damnation. For you, daughters of Jerusalem, who accompany Me to Calvary, gather up every drop of this same blood, and be well persuaded that if it demands vengeance against hardened sinners, it will no less demand mercy for the penitent.

After having read attentively, in this mysterious book which was seen in vision by the prophet, all that can furnish us with matter for compassion or fear, let us examine the motives it supplies for praising God and rendering Him eternal thanks for all the blessings we have received or for which we hope, and which are contained in Jesus crucified: these are the *canticles* of which the prophet speaks. The wounds of this Man of Sorrows are so many characters which signify the charity, mercy and infinite liberality of God, the obedience, the sweetness and marvellous patience of the Saviour, His zeal for our salvation, the inestimable riches of His grace and glory. By His *crown of thorns* we can judge of what price is that crown which He prepares for us in Heaven; His *thirst* and His *nakedness* should make us think of the happiness which is ours in being able to drink from the living fountains of grace, and of clothing ourselves with the robe of charity; the *wounds* of His hands, feet and side show us the love He bears us, that love which is so firm and constant that in order never to forget us, He has written us not only in His hands but even in His heart, having no other desire but to unite us to Himself by a perpetual love, and incessantly exhorting us never to break asunder a bond so sacred.

But it is not enough only to read this book of which we speak, for Ezechiel says it is to be *eaten*[8] and devoured: Open then your mouth and eat it all up, striving to incorporate it into your own being by charity and to transform yourself into it by imitation: *in thy mouth* it shall be *as sweet as honey, but when* thou hast eaten it thy *belly shall be bitter.*[9] For the mysteries it contains are pleasant to taste and sweet to speak of; but it is hard to practise what they command; although, by dint of thinking of them, the difficulties are smoothed away and mortification itself becomes agreeable.

My Saviour, with Thine own blood Thou hast written these *lamentations, canticles* and *threats,* teach me to read them in the same spirit with which Thou hast written them; enkindle so ardently Thy love in my heart that out of love I may lament my sins; out of love I may dread Thy judgements; out of love I may praise Thee also for Thy benefits; out of the same love I may hope for Thy supreme reward: that by loving and imitating what I read in Thy book, I may attain to the enjoyment of what I desire.

The sum of all that we have here said is briefly expressed thus by St Bonaventure:[10] Christ our Lord, he says, in His passion, opened the seven seals of the book which St John saw sealed; for He laid open seven different mysteries which till then were deeply hidden from men, the wisdom, namely,

[8] Ez 3:1
[9] Cf. Apoc 10:9
[10] *De incend. amoris,* Part 3

and the admirable perfection of God, the value of man's soul, the vanity of all things earthly, the horrors of Hell, the joys of Paradise, the loathsomeness of sin and the excellence of virtue; moreover we may say that Christ crucified is a book unsealed. For all the deceits and errors with which the minds of men were encumbered concerning these seven things were exposed by Him, so that henceforth we may read and usefully meditate on all that this book contains, to bring forth in due season these seven fruits, or others that we may obtain from it ourselves.

II. Of the resemblance effected by love

It will now be necessary to explain in some detail the qualities and excellences of divine and unitive love, to which the reading and eating of this book of Christ crucified invites us; from His cross He says to us, more by deeds than words, that saying of the Spouse in the Canticle: *Put me as a seal upon thy heart, as a seal upon thy arm, for love is strong as death, jealousy as hard as Hell, the lamps thereof are fire and flames. Many waters cannot quench charity, neither can the floods drown it: if a man should give all the substance of his house for love, he shall despise it as nothing.*[11] Under these figures of seal, death, the grave, Hell, fire and floods, the Holy Spirit admirably expresses the qualities of perfect love.

Of these the first, as we began to say above,[12] is to cause a great likeness and conformity in all things, interior and exterior, between the lover and his Lord; he places Him as a seal upon his heart and arm, as He is upon the cross. For when has He ever appeared more clearly in the likeness of a seal than in the mystery of His passion, when the eternal Father sealed Him

[11] Cant. 8:6
[12] Chap. 2

by the hands of lictors and executioners? as He said by His prophet: *I will grave the graving thereof, saith the Lord of Hosts*;[13] that is, engraving deep lines in His hands and feet, piercing His head with many thorns, opening His back with many scourges, and lastly perforating His heart with a spear; *For I will make* Him, as he says by another prophet, *as a signet,* in a beautiful ring, *for I have chosen* Him that I may impress His likeness on all My elect.[14]

No one is ignorant that a seal and the thing marked with it closely resemble one another: in both may be seen the same design, yet always with this difference, that the seal is made of gold or silver or some precious stone; that it is fashioned very skilfully, and being cut into the substance, the form remains distinct for a long time: on the other hand, the impression we make with the seal is quickly obliterated, because it is impressed on wax or something of that nature, and often it is not well formed, or only half completed, or crooked, not by the fault of the seal, but by the clumsiness of him who applies it, or who uses some matter which is too hard to take the impression. This is how Jesus crucified, that model of all perfection, and His elect ought to resemble each other; since no one is holy except because *God has predestinated him to be made conformable to the image of His Son.*[15] The difference between them lies in this, that Jesus Christ being God and man, possesses every virtue in a sovereign degree, without any possibility of losing them or their suffering any diminution or deterioration. He possessed them all from the first moment of His life: but they were hidden in the depths of His soul, and in order that they might shine forth before the world in all their splendour, it was necessary that His sacred body should be pierced with wounds

[13] Zach 3:9
[14] Agg 2:14
[15] Rom 8:29

and that, as says St Bernard,[16] we might perceive through these openings all that was in His most secret heart. Should we be astonished, adds the holy doctor, that through so many wounds He has revealed the bowels of His love and mercy, that He has displayed His humility, His patience, His obedience, all His virtues, in order to imprint their likeness on the souls of the just? The pity is that this image is impressed on wax, and that it is immediately obliterated unless God Himself takes in hand to conserve it. Often, too, those who receive it do not receive it in all its perfection; there may be many defects, not that anything is wanting in the seal or that Christ our Lord does not desire with all His heart to see them perfect in every virtue, but because they are not well-disposed and because they neglect to do, with the help of God, what depends upon themselves, which is themselves to apply this seal to their arms and heart, by conforming their actions and works to those of Jesus Christ.

But we must not stop here: Jesus Christ must be sole Master of our heart, He must possess it entirely, every other must be banished for ever. Mark well, then, beloved soul, He says, that as wax cannot take two impressions at the same time (for one would immediately obliterate the other): so a faithful and chaste spouse cannot cherish two loves contrary the one to the other, but must set her whole heart on Christ her only husband and spouse,[17] loving Him with her whole heart and soul and mind and strength,[18] as the commandment of love prescribes. Beware, therefore, lest thou sign thy heart with the seal of the world, or of anti-Christ, which is the image of pride, cupidity and sensuality; but seal it with the signet of My life, which is the image of humility, poverty and purity of body and soul.

---

[16] *Patet arcanum cordis per foramina corporis; Quid in vulnera per viscera pateat.* Serm. 61 in *Cant.*
[17] Cf. 2 Cor 11:2
[18] Ex 6:5

Thou oughtest to place Me as a seal upon thy heart and upon thy arm, that thou mayest love Me as I love thee, live with My life, and unite thyself to Me as I desire to unite Myself to thee; neither canst thou conserve My likeness and image unless I assist thee to do so.

But lest thou shouldst neglect to carry out what I command, I have added *threats* and canticles of *woe;* for I wish you to know that *love is strong as death, jealousy hard as Hell;* which is as much as to say that love when angered is strong and terrible as death itself, but jealousy is as hard and pitiless as Hell; if the spouse do not keep faith, the more she has been loved, the more will she be contemned as faithless and ungrateful; however loudly she may cry for mercy, I will not listen, but unless she return I shall condemn her, as she deserves, to eternal punishment.

Most chaste Spouse of souls, it is most just that Thou alone shouldst be the seal with which they are stamped, nor any other image admitted which would efface Thine. But how can I place Thee as a seal upon my soul, since that is Thy work rather than mine? For if it is mine, it is so only by Thy assistance; place Thyself therefore as a seal upon my heart, impress the living image of Thy virtues upon it accurately and completely, blotting out for ever every figure of detestable vice. I offer Thee my heart as soft wax, apt and ready to receive Thy seal: do Thou apply it and impress it deeply, so that the image may appear exact and clear, even though it cost me suffering and labour. For if it has cost Thee so much to be made the seal of Thy elect, is it too much that they also should suffer somewhat to be stamped with it? From henceforward I will say with the Apostle: *That I may live to God, with Christ I am nailed to the cross.*[19] Christ crucified shall be my seal, the image of mortification; what He has borne in His body, I will bear in mine; the thorns with which His head was crowned shall crown mine also; the nails

[19] Gal 2:19

which transfixed His hands and feet, shall transfix mine also: *God forbid that I should glory, save in the cross of our Lord Jesus Christ,*[20] by whose love I live, as one affixed to the cross, and *I bear the marks of the Lord Jesus in my body,*[21] *crucifying my flesh with its vices and concupiscences.*[22]

III. Of the mortification which love produces

Let us now pass on to another property of divine love which gives it power to enter and reign alone in the heart: *it is strong as death.* It resists, it conquers, it puts to death, so to speak, every affection which is purely natural or vicious, yet with a certain distinction. For it imitates death, which takes away the life of every living creature by dissolving the union, however long it may have existed, between soul and body; but it does not take it away in the same degree from reasonable creatures as from the irrational. In brute beasts whensoever it separates the soul from the body, it utterly destroys both these without any possibility of their being reunited: in men, it cannot cause the annihilation of the soul, which is immortal; it only separates it from the body, so that being delivered from this prison it may live as a pure spirit, in perfect liberty, no longer subject to the laws of the flesh.

For this reason perfect charity is as strong as death: it exterminates from the heart every affection which is ever so little contrary to it. If its affections are evil, if they have their root in self-love, or love that is carnal and worldly, it annihilates them altogether, and even if they have struck very deep roots, it tears them out; in their place it gives a horror of every mortal sin and vicious habit, a firm determination never to commit

[20] Gal 6:14
[21] Gal 6:17
[22] Cf. Gal 5:24

even a single deliberate venial sin, and in order not to relapse into former disorders, a careful guard against the very first movement which might lead to sin.

But if it is only a question of affections purely human and natural, such as the love of parents, of health, of life, divine love is not accustomed to destroy them; it is content to cut off by mortification all that is sensual, but what is good it preserves, cherishes, perfects, and changes in this way feelings that were merely human into others perfectly pure and spiritual. So that if we desire health, if we fear sickness, if we love our parents, if we rejoice in prosperity, if we are saddened by adversity, it is no longer by the movement of a natural passion, it is from the principle of the love of God, in whom and for whom we love all that He wills and hate all that He wills not.

Of this we have a striking example in Jesus Christ, who for the salvation of sinners overcame all the feelings of nature; I do not say those which are criminal, for He could not have any such, and although He suffered unendurable anguish, He was never tempted to impatience: I only speak of those which are the common effect of human infirmity, fear, sadness, love of life; He never ceased to struggle against these throughout the long night of His passion; in the end He bore off the palm of victory, saying to His Father: *Not My will but Thine be done.*[23] He offered Himself courageously to death, and it was necessary that He should do so, for otherwise neither the world nor Hell itself could have taken away His life.

O love strong as death! if you have had such power over the All-powerful, how much more ought you to have over weak and mortal men! My soul, if love has been able to nail to a cross the only Son of God, shall it be too much for you to desire to be attached to another? Think no longer of anything but of carrying till death the image of Jesus suffering, that you may

---

[23] Lk 22:42

live as if crucified and entirely dead to the world for love of Him. But do not imagine that victorious love will stop here: *Jealousy is as hard as Hell,* or the grave, which shows another of its qualities, of which we have now to speak.

The grave and Hell are the two most hard and cruel enemies we have after death. The grave exercises its cruelty over the body, for it strips it of everything and consumes even that which death had spared; it reduces to powder the flesh, veins and arteries without anything remaining of the many different component parts save the dry bones; in this manner it carries out with the utmost severity the sentence pronounced against Adam and all his posterity: *Dust thou art and into dust thou shalt return.*[24] But Hell torments the guilty soul and causes it to suffer horrible punishments for its offences. Neither Hell nor the grave know what it is to pardon anyone; once they have laid hold on their prey, never will they desist until the full penalty has been paid.

Divine love also, though opposed to all violence, yet has its severity for those who love; for not only does it stifle in them all irregular motions, but for their greater perfection, it despoils them of their riches, it causes them to abandon father and mother, relations and friends; it drags them from the world to bury them in religion or some desert spot, that henceforth they may live for God alone. It inspires them with a mortal hatred of themselves and with generous desires of expiating their past faults by rigorous penances, of abasing themselves to the dust and below the feet of all; of even enduring the pains of Hell to make satisfaction to God, should He require it. Thus does it lead them to imitate Jesus, whose jealousy was for Him as hard as Hell, according to that saying of David in His person: *The zeal* (or jealousy) *of thy house hath eaten me up;*[25] consuming

[24] Gen 3:19
[25] Ps 68:10

Him little by little. For with Him it consumed all His possessions, His honour, His happiness; it caused Him to die upon the cross in nakedness and shame; lastly, it placed His body all covered with wounds in the grave and it obliged His soul to descend into Hell, that is to say Limbo, not indeed there to suffer torments, since He had already suffered these to the full in satisfaction for the sins of men, but in order to experience this humiliation also and to set at liberty the souls of the saints who had already for so long waited for their liberator.

Would to God my soul might die this happy death and enter into that desirable sepulchre, there to be enclosed and sealed with the seal of the Beloved. Only Love of my heart, *let my soul die the death of the just, and my last end be like to them,*[26] that *my life* may *be* buried and *hidden with Christ in* Thee, my *God,* for ever.[27]

IV. Of the fortitude, both for action and for suffering, which love engenders

In order to show how the death and sepulture which are the fruit of divine love produce in him who loves a noble and excellent life, the Holy Spirit adds that this love is like a lamp always burning with fire and flames.[28] This shows that it sheds on all sides its light and heat, by heroic actions, by ardent affections, which do not lie on the earth like coals, but rise to Heaven like flames and which draw to themselves those hearts which are detached from all that is earthly, to unite them to their Beloved by the bonds of perpetual charity. It is not then without reason that it is compared to the flame of a

[26] Num 23:10
[27] Cf. Col 3:3
[28] Cf. Cant 8:6

lamp, which cannot give light unless its oil is consumed; for it employs its whole being in the service of this lovable Saviour who was Himself wholly consumed on the cross and Who, from Mount Calvary where He offered Himself as a holocaust, has shed burning rays throughout the world, that He might set all hearts on fire.

If thy enemy be hungry, give him to eat: if he thirst, give him water to drink: for thou shalt heap hot coals upon his head, says the Wise Man;[29] what is this but to sacrifice honour, goods and life itself to deliver him from death, even death eternal? Can anyone deny that Christ nailed to the cross was like a furnace filled with as many hot coals as He suffered pains, as He has heaped benefits upon us, as He has delivered us from evils by His sufferings? He heaps all these burning coals on *our* heads that He may soften our hearts, and win them by so many benefits; in order also to oblige us to love with all our strength Him who has loved us so much.

Most sweet Saviour, Who hast made for Thyself a pyre out of Thy cross, and Who dost say to me: *I am come to cast fire on the earth, and what will I, but that it be kindled?*[30] enkindle my soul, which is but cold and barren earth, set it on fire with Thy divine love; cause it to be quite carried away by the motion of this celestial fire, or else, transforming itself into a flame, may it be wholly joined to Thine, becoming one same spirit with Thine.

Notice that it is not without mystery that the Holy Spirit compares love to death, the grave and Hell, four insatiable things which *never say: Enough:*[31] for he who loves God with his whole soul counts as nothing all that he does and suffers for Him; he is never content with himself; he desires always to grow, always to advance, always to be making fresh progress.

[29] Prov 25:21, 22, cf. Rom 12:20
[30] Lk 12:49
[31] Prov 30:15. Cf. Ricard., Tract. *De Charit. vulnerata*

If he dies to created things by an entire mortification of his appetites, he still believes he ought to die yet more: if he is buried, if he hides himself from the eyes of the world by humility, he yet strives to bury and hide himself still more deeply; if he punishes himself for his sins, from day to day he adds still more to his penances; if he is a *burning and a shining light*,[32] if he enlightens and enkindles his neighbour by holy and edifying deeds, he desires ever to increase in fervour and in light. To whatever degree of perfection he may have attained, he seeks to raise himself yet higher, and will never desist nor ask for repose until he shall be united to his Beloved for ever.

But nothing better portrays the excellence and strength of divine love than the words which the Holy Spirit now adds: *Many waters cannot quench charity, neither can the floods drown it.*[33] From them we see its invincible firmness and constancy in the midst of all the trials as well interior as exterior by which it seems as if it must be overwhelmed, from whatever side they may come, whether from heaven like the rain or from the earth like floods. These waters, these floods are only like drops of water which, being cast into a furnace, rather increase than diminish its heat. For indeed, the more charity finds itself burdened with labours, the more is it fortified, and in order to acquire new strength, it desires fresh pains; because it is ever straining after that highest point of perfection which consists in the desire *to lay down one's life* for the Beloved.[34]

If this virtue has shone forth anywhere, it was in Christ our Saviour on whom it poured a deluge of waters, and of waters that were of extreme bitterness; of these the Psalmist spoke, saying: *The waters are come in even unto my soul. I stick fast in the mire of the deep… I am come into the depth of the sea: and a*

[32] Jn 5:35
[33] Cant 8:7
[34] Cf. Jn 15:13

tempest hath overwhelmed me.[35] Yet was He never submerged; the fire with which His heart was consumed, instead of dying down, only burnt more vehemently. By the mouth of the same prophet[36] He complained that during His passion He was as if besieged by an army of men as fierce and cruel as *bulls, dogs, unicorns* and *lions:* so many enemies fell upon Him simultaneously and attacked Him principally in five places and five separate times, namely in the Garden, in the house of Caiphas, in the palace of Herod, in Pilate's Praetorium and on Mount Calvary; everywhere His charity was unconquerable, everywhere it carried off the victory. The only vengeance He took was by heaping up benefits, He prayed for those who ill-treated Him, He made excuse for them to His Father, He even offered His blood and His life for them, which is the most certain and remarkable proof of perfect love; since, as says the Apostle, *scarcely for a just man will one die: but...* Christ *commendeth His charity towards us: because when we were yet sinners* He *died for us;*[37] neither the *many waters* of our sins could *overwhelm* His charity nor the *floods* of the most terrible torments *quench* nor *drown* it.

After this, is it possible that we shall not love Him in the same manner as He has loved us? Shall we not serve joyfully, and even at the risk of our life, if need be, Him who has redeemed us at the price of His blood? Shall we fear to say with St Paul: *Who then shall separate us from the love of Christ? Shall tribulation? or distress? or famine? or nakedness? or danger? or persecution? or the sword?... But in all these things we overcome, because of Him who hath loved us. For I am sure that neither death, nor life, nor Angels, nor Principalities, nor Powers, nor things present, nor things to come, nor might, nor height, nor*

[35] Ps 68:1-3
[36] Ps 21:13, 17, 22
[37] Cf. Rom 5:7-9

depth, nor any other creature shall be able to separate us from the love of God, which is in Christ Jesus;[38] that is to say, neither the love which God has for us, nor the love we have for God; because the charity of God is unchangeable and in consideration of the merits of His Son He communicates to us a love like to His own.

All-powerful Redeemer, make me to love Thee as Thou lovest me, so that I may ever be eager for reproaches for love of Thee, as Thou hast been for love of me: unite my heart so closely to Thine that both may burn with the selfsame fire, so that whensoever my enemies come about me to attack me, all their efforts will be useless, since I can never be vanquished as long as Thou art with me.

V. *Of the generosity of love*

The last and most noble property of love divine is expressed in these words: *If a man should give all the substance of his house for love, he shall despise it as nothing.*[39] In these words we see how precious a thing is charity and that he who possesses it should spare nothing in order to keep it: this esteem will be shown principally in three ways.

The *first* is, that to obtain this gift, a man will give all he possesses, reserving nothing at all for himself.

The *second* is more perfect, in that, when he has given all, even though the thing may be of great value in itself, yet it shall seem to him of little worth, and whatever he shall give, he will despise it as nothing.

The *third* is more perfect still, that not only shall he esteem himself to have given little, although he has given much, but

---

[38] Rom 8:35-39
[39] Cant 8:7

also, when what he has given is of great price, he shall be willing to be judged mad and a fool for having given it. This is more clearly shown in the Septuagint version, which reads: *If a man shall give his whole life for love, despising shall they despise him.*[40] For one who does not know what it is to love will judge to be folly what he sees done by a true lover: moreover he will contemn and despise him.

These three things shone forth in an admirable degree in Jesus Christ crucified, of Whom by excellence it is said: *If a man shall give.*[41] For although it is true that love and zeal for our salvation reduced Him to such a condition that He could truly say: *I am a worm and no man: the reproach of men and the outcast of the people;*[42] yet even in this He showed that He is perfect man, governing all His human faculties with the highest reason and discretion, although not man only but the God-man, of whom the Apostle says:[43] *Being rich, He became poor, for your sakes;* out of love for us He despoiled Himself of everything, He died naked upon the cross; His whole life, from the day of His birth till that of His death, was spent in the continual exercise of charity towards others; He did many wonderful and stupendous things; He underwent extraordinary sufferings; He did not even grudge life itself for those He loved, and to crown His generosity He nourishes them day by day with His own body and blood, as we are about to see. But what is more astonishing than all is, that after having undergone so many labours and sufferings, it should all seem to Him as nothing, so that He would willingly endure as much again were it necessary. For even to remain entire centuries in such

---

[40] *Si dederit homo omnem vitam suam pro dilectione, despectione despicient eum.*
[41] Ps 86:5, *Homo natus est in ea.*
[42] Ps 21:7
[43] 2 Cor 8:9

torments, to give His life a thousand times, to endure every kind of pain, would not be enough fully to content a love as insatiable as His. He offered Himself to undergo it all from the first moment of His coming into this world, although He could not be ignorant that instead of praises and thanks He would receive nothing but outrages, and that the mystery of the cross would be *to the Jews a stumbling-block, and unto the Gentiles foolishness;*[44] an object of derision to those who could not understand either the love or the wisdom which prompted Him to deliver himself up to death, as much for the glory of His Father as for the salvation of sinners.

Faithful souls, animated by this example which they ought to keep continually before their eyes, will conceive such generous desires of imitating their divine Master that there will be nothing which they will not be ready to give with their whole heart to obtain and preserve this gift of charity. This is the treasure of the Gospel, that precious *treasure hidden in a field, which a man having found, for joy thereof goeth and selleth all that he hath, and buyeth that field;*[45] it is that inestimable *pearl* to obtain which the merchant *sold all that he had and bought it.* It is of such price that merely to acquire it, religious renounce the world and the martyrs offer themselves to death; lastly, the saints have such esteem for it that they feel unable to live unless they love, and if they desire to prolong their lives, it is that they may love yet more Him who has loved them from all eternity. And even after they have done all they could and given all they have they reckon they have neither done much nor given much, because in comparison of divine charity *all gold in comparison of her is as a little sand, and silver in respect to her shall be counted as clay,*[46] all the treasures the world can contain are worth nothing.

[44] 1 Cor 1:3
[45] Mt 13:44
[46] Wis 7:9

And although they are aware that by despoiling themselves of everything they expose themselves to contempt, they reckon little of that, because, like Moses, they esteem *the reproach of Christ greater riches than the treasure of the Egyptians*;[47] they admire as great wisdom what the world rejects as folly; they bear in mind that sentence of Job: *the simplicity of the just man is laughed to scorn; the lamp despised in the thoughts of the rich is ready for the time appointed.*[48] The burning lamp is, as we have seen, a symbol of that charity which the Spirit of sanctity sheds abroad in the hearts of the just: the great men of the world make little account of it, because, in the judgement of worldlings, it gives neither light nor heat; but when the time determined by Providence shall come, it will burn with such brilliance that those who before despised the simplicity of the good, will begin to admire their wisdom and praise their conduct. Then, convinced at last of the truth, they will cry out with tears in their eyes and despair in their hearts: *we fools esteemed their life madness, and their end without honour;* now is our error unmasked, for *behold how they are numbered among the children of God, and their lot is among the saints.*[49]

Christ our Lord before Caiaphas was one of these despised lamps, yet while they were contemning Him He boldly declared: *Hereafter you shall see the Son of man sitting on the right hand of the power of God, and coming in the clouds of heaven*[50] with great majesty and manifesting His divinity, which was at that time concealed from the eyes of His enemies, although to His friends it was ever apparent. For on the candlestick of the cross He so burned and shone that by many He was recognised and proclaimed as the Son of the living God and the King of

[47] Heb 11:26
[48] Job 12:4, 5
[49] Wis 5:4, 5
[50] Mt 26:64

Paradise, so that there began immediately to be fulfilled what He Himself had foretold: *I, if I be lifted up from the earth, will draw all things to Myself,*[51] exalting them above the earth, that where I am they also may be.

O fire of infinite love, which drawest all things to Thyself that Thou mayest transform them into Thee by love and imitation! Thou drawest to Thyself their memory, that they may ever think of Thee, their understanding, that they may believe in Thee and know Thee, their will, that they may love Thee; their powers and senses that they may obey Thee, their body and soul that they may be occupied in Thy service; their fortune, honour, pleasure, health and life, that all these may be instruments for Thy glory. But what wonder that all things are drawn to Thee, since all things are found in Thee? Draw me, Lord, to Thee, that I may love Thee as Thou lovest me; make my spirit like to Thine upon the cross; let me share one cross with Thee, that with Thee I may be fixed to it by the nails of love so securely that neither the prosperity of life nor the bitterness of death may separate me from the cross until by it Thou shalt unite me to Thyself in eternal glory. Amen.

---

[51] Jn 12:32

Chapter VI

How we may acquire a loving knowledge of Jesus Christ in the Most Holy Sacrament, by the consideration of seven marvellous things contained in it; and of the heroic virtues He exercises therein and examples of perfection which He gives to all the faithful.

OF ALL THE MEANS which we have here below of acquiring in an eminent degree the loving and unitive knowledge of God our Lord and of His Son Jesus Christ, the most noble, the most efficacious, the most powerful and the most proportioned to our weakness is the august Sacrament of the Eucharist, in which the Saviour Himself dwells and where He is exposed before our eyes like an open book. This book is all spiritual and has three most excellent properties.

The *first* is that it furnishes us with very ample matter for useful reflection on the whole life of our Lord, from His incarnation to His ascension. It is indeed intended to bring it to our memory according to these words of Jesus Himself to His Apostles: *This do ye, as often as ye shall drink, for the commemoration of Me;*[1] David had already foretold the same thing when he said: *He hath made a remembrance of his wonderful works, being a merciful and gracious Lord: He hath given food to them that fear Him.*[2]

The *second* is that it imprints in the depth of our hearts all the doctrine it contains, because it enters profoundly into the

[1] 1 Cor 11:24
[2] Ps 110:4

soul, which, being a divine bread, it transforms into itself. It is no new thing that God wills us not only to read His books, but also to eat them, that their virtue may be communicated to the eater; in this is fulfilled to the letter what the Author of the Sacrament Himself said one day to the beloved disciple: *Take the book and eat it up.*[3] Hence it is that by receiving this Sacrament we are marvellously instructed, enkindled and transformed into Jesus Christ, true God and true man, and filled with a loving knowledge of His Godhead and His humanity; whence proceeds that very perfect union of our spirit with His which is the end and principal effect of the Sacrament.

Now there are two ways of being nourished and profiting by this book: the one is *sacramental,* when we draw near to the holy table and eat in very deed the body of the Saviour; the other *spiritual,* when, by dint of reading, meditating and ruminating on those things which it contains, we are enabled to produce lively acts of faith concerning them. Yet although it is a book carefully and firmly sealed with *seven seals,*[4] which are very difficult to break, if our faith is strong enough to open it, we may discover seven great marvels, which will greatly assist us in obtaining a true knowledge of the divine perfections.

And in order that no one should despair of understanding them, this mysterious book has a *third* property, which is that it contains within itself Him who has written it, and to whom it belongs to declare its true meaning; for it contains in very truth the Lamb of God, who opened and explained that other book which was seen by St John in the Apocalypse; so that He is in a certain ineffable manner both the book, and its interpretation and the spiritual nourishment to be found in it. All this may be found enclosed in the species of a little bread, according to these words of Isaias: *The Lord will give you spare bread and*

[3] Apoc 10:9; Ez 3:1
[4] Apoc 5:1

short water: and will not cause thy teacher to flee away from thee any more, and thy eyes shall see thy teacher.[5] For although this prophecy chiefly regards the time when the Son of God, in visible form, should preach to the world His new law, which is briefly contained in the two precepts of the love of God and of our neighbour and which leads men to Heaven by the narrow way;[6] we may also apply it to the Sacrament of the Eucharist, in which this Man-God is contained in a very small space, in the tiniest particle of a host, in the least drop of consecrated wine. In passing, let us remark that in the chalice a little water is mingled with the wine, in memory of the sufferings and pains which Jesus Christ had to undergo during His passion to expiate our sins and to show us, by example rather than by words, how to follow the narrow path of mortification, and to inscribe in our hearts a kind of abridgement of the law of charity.

And beyond all this, He dwells so continually with us that He never leaves us; and God, who has given Him to us as our Master, will not permit that we should be separated from Him. It is true that after His resurrection, He rose like an eagle to the highest Heaven, where we cannot see Him as He is; yet, nonetheless, He has not abandoned the earth, He dwells in the midst of us, and will do so till the end of the world; our eyes see Him though but dimly and through the species of bread and wine. Trusting ourselves then to the help of this sovereign Master, let us begin to meditate on the seven miracles which God performs and which faith reveals to us in this book of life, this living bread: we will reflect also on the admirable virtues it contains which are practised by Him who has instituted this Sacrament, that the treasures of His wisdom and bounty may shine forth in us. But because in the first place we have great need to fortify our faith, let us call to mind those cele-

---

[5] Isaias 30:20
[6] Cf. St Jerome, *ibid*

brated words of St Augustine:[7] *If you seek to understand, it will no longer be admirable: and if you seek its fellow, it will lose its singularity.* Let us confess that God can do things which we can never comprehend; for in such wonders the only reason for what is done is the infinite power of Him who operates.

I. Of the union of God and man with the species of bread and wine

The *first* miracle which takes place in the sacrament of the altar is the union of two things in themselves very unlike, I mean the body and blood of Jesus Christ with the species of bread and wine. For what could be more admirable than to see the Lord of Heaven, the King of glory closely united with things which are low, base and earthly? This is that admirable thing spoken of by the prophet Zacharias saying: *For what is the good thing of him, and what is his beautiful thing, but the corn of the elect, and wine springing forth virgins?*[8] O marvel of eternal Wisdom, which has found means to conceal under the accidents of bread and wine all the goodness and all the beauty of God, of joining to a little bread the salvation, the life and the eternal happiness of mankind, of giving to wine the power to produce virgins! But leaving aside these two last wonders, of which we shall speak of elsewhere, let us treat only of the first, and let us see how the only-begotten Son of God, under the

---

[7] Epist. 3 *ad Volusianum. Si ratio quaeritur, non erit admirabilis: et si quaeritur exemplum, non erit singularis.* For an adequate rendering of this phrase, we should have to read it in its original context. Its meaning here evidently is: That from whatever point of view you consider the Holy Eucharist, its essence, signification, being or working, you will find nothing (considering God's infinite power, wisdom and love) which need surprise your faith, or seem too much for it. (Transl.)

[8] Zach 9:17

species of bread and wine, gives to us all He has that is good and beautiful, either in Himself or outside Himself, either in body or in soul, in every kind of supernatural gift and perfection which proceed from the uncreated goodness and beauty.

For it is in this august Sacrament that the Divinity, that is, essential Goodness and Beauty, resides: there is found the most beautiful and perfect union which divine Wisdom could devise, that namely of the Eternal Word with a human nature; not only with the soul, but also with the flesh and blood of which this sacred humanity is composed. In this Sacrament again we revere the most beautiful of all created things in the world of spirits, that is, the soul of Christ our Lord, which shines among the celestial hierarchies like a sun among the stars. There also we adore the body of Him whom David with good reason called the *most beautiful of the sons of men*,[9] the body which contains so lovely a soul, whose veins are filled with that most pure blood which has washed away the sins of the world. It is there that we see and admire the plenitude of grace, virtues and other gifts which God has communicated and which He will eternally continue to communicate to His creatures; because Jesus alone possesses all the treasures of the wisdom and knowledge of God,[10] because He has in a sovereign degree all the light of glory, because He governs the universe with absolute power, because He enjoys an infinite number of other advantages, and because from Him, as from an inexhaustible source, stream forth into His own all He has to give of beauty and goodness.

Lastly, as according to St Thomas,[11] everything that is good is the object of love, while all that is beautiful is the object of knowledge, and as these two acts are the most perfect of those

---

[9] Ps 44:3
[10] Cf. Col 2:3
[11] St Thomas Aquinas, Summa Theologiae, Ia, q. 5, a. 4, ad 1

produced by the contemplative life; if it is also true that we have in the blessed Eucharist all that is good and beautiful in God, we have as well all that we can desire, all that can satisfy our will and our understanding and still the longings of our heart: we find there all that is praised in the Sacred Scriptures, all that is to be admired in the most noble creatures, all this perfection we find in the highest possible degree. Yet it is all hidden under the veil of the accidents of bread and wine, to make known to us the profound humility of the Son of God, who, willing to give the world a rare example of this virtue, covers the splendour of His majesty with so poor and despicable a veil. O miracle of the wisdom and charity of God! The Apostle marvels that the only-begotten Son of the Most High, *who, being in the form of God, thought it not robbery to be equal with God, but emptied Himself, taking the form of a servant, being made in the likeness of men,*[12] hid the glory of His divinity under the vileness of our humanity. Shall we not then wonder that this same God, made man, wills to abase Himself on our altars so far as to take the form of bread and wine, to clothe Himself with the accidents of these corruptible substances, and to hide under so fragile a veil all the glory of His divinity and His humanity?

My God, let the most sublime hierarchies of angels praise Thee for that being infinitely beautiful and infinitely great, Thou hast not let this appear! The more Thou seekest to hide and humiliate Thyself, the more do I admire Thee, the more I love Thee. Well didst Thou know when Thou didst institute this Sacrament that many, going no further than the outward appearance and realising only what their eyes could show them, would despise Thee, would tread Thee under foot, as common bread. Thou didst know it, just as when making Thyself man Thou didst know that many would never distinguish Thee from

[12] Phil 2:7

the rest of mankind, and that instead of honouring Thee, they would heap upon Thee every imaginable insult. But the infinite charity towards us with which Thy heart has always been filled made Thee resolve to accept all these humiliations. Thou wert silent, thou didst feign not to see them, Thou sufferedst in silence, Thou didst take no vengeance for all the injuries they did Thee, so much didst Thou desire that we should learn from Thee to be meek and humble of heart. O humility! O inconceivable meekness! O Master of Heaven, who ceasest not to tell us, rather by deeds than by words: *Learn of Me, for I am meek and humble of heart;*[13] teach me to hide whatever virtues and talents I possess as Thou hidest Thy divine perfections; to suffer my humiliations patiently, as Thou dost suffer Thine; make me rejoice, Lord, to be esteemed for what I am worth, to be despised as I deserve, since Thou didst rejoice to be unknown and not to be honoured as Thou didst merit to be.

II. Of the miracle of transubstantiation, and how the accidents of bread and wine remain without the substance which naturally sustains them

This first miracle is accompanied by several others no less surprising, in which are resplendent truths and examples of a sublime perfection. The *second* of these is that of *transubstantiation,* when the substance of bread and wine is changed into the substance of the body and blood of Christ our Lord. Other prodigious examples of miraculous changes have been performed, such as the rod of Moses which turned into a serpent[14] and the water into wine at Cana;[15] but these were not

[13] Mt 11:29
[14] Ex 7:10
[15] Jn 2

invisible changes like this one, where it is only the substance of the bread and wine which are changed, and in which Christ our Lord places Himself under the sacramental species without destroying them, as He entered into the womb of the Blessed Virgin without detriment to her virginity. Nevertheless, though invisible, it is not the less veritable. "If birds," says St Thomas,[16] "by natural heat can convert into living flesh the yolk of an egg without breaking the shell, should we be astonished that the Son of God, by His almighty power, should change the substance of bread into His body without destroying the accidents?"

This marvel, being so deeply hidden, is no slight test of our faith and may be taken to represent certain secret changes which the right hand of the Most High, who is with us, operates in us, although nothing appears outwardly; as when He changes our heart without any alteration in our body, or when in the deep places of our soul He converts feelings which are natural and human into those which are supernatural and divine. So that, just as the flesh of the Son of God penetrates the accidents and takes the place of the bread and wine: so the spirit of the Son of God penetrates all our powers and takes the place of our spirit. From this it results that, being animated not by our own proper spirit but by His, we can say with the Apostle: *I live, now not I; but Christ liveth in me*[17] and makes me live by His grace.

All this appears still more clearly in the *third* miracle, which is a consequence of the second, and which consists in the separation of two things which nature has united very closely, the accidents and the substance of the bread and the wine. By an unparalleled example, God conserves these accidents without the substance which ought naturally to sustain them; so that they remain suspended like a building with no foundation.

[16] St Thomas Aquinas, *Opusc.* 58, ch. 11 *et seq.*
[17] Gal 2:20

And although he who communicates sees the colour, perceives the odour and tastes the savour of the bread and wine, yet he must believe what his faith teaches him, that the substance of these things is no longer there, and that Jesus Christ, having taken the place of the bread and wine, has separated the accidents from the substance, making them subsist by themselves, contrary to the order of nature. Thus, in the presence of the Ark of the Covenant, the type of the Eucharist, did God divide the waters of the Jordan, holding back one part, while the other, continuing its course, flowed on to lose itself in the Dead Sea.[18]

What the divine wisdom desires to teach us by this prodigy is that the adorable Sacrament, if we receive it worthily, will raise us to such a pitch of perfection that we shall no longer be held by any attachment to any creature, not even to those for whom naturally we ought to have most affection, being well persuaded that if we find no support in created things, we shall always find it in our Creator, for Whose love we shall be able to live, if necessary, separated from our brethren, our parents, our friends, and any others on whom we might depend. For, as the Son of God, according to what He Himself has told us in the Gospel, *came not to send peace upon earth, but the sword,*[19] and to set division between those who are hindered from serving Him as they ought by affections which are too human, if not sinful: in the same way the eternal Word, this *living word more piercing than any two-edged sword,*[20] comes into our souls to separate fleshly affections from spiritual, to kill the flesh in order that the spirit may live.

But notice that after the consecration, the substance of the bread and wine being changed, there remains under the sacramental species Jesus Christ alone, for He could not suffer

[18] Josue 3:13
[19] Mt 10:34
[20] Hebr 4:12

any other substance to be there but that of His own body and blood: thus every Christian, after Holy Communion, ought to offer himself as a holocaust to his Lord, and consume in the fire of charity all his earthly affections, so that, his soul being completely purified, Jesus Christ alone may live in him. For, to use the words of the prophet, *the bed is straitened, so that one must fall out, and a short covering cannot cover both,*[21] especially if one push the other, and there is a continual war between them. It is a horrible sacrilege to wish to place on the same altar *the Ark of the Lord and the idol of Dagon.*[22] Whosoever therefore wishes to receive his Saviour worthily should begin by exterminating from his soul all inordinate love of creatures, for it is not fitting that he should receive Him only in passing and for a moment, but for always: he must have a firm desire never to be separated from Him, and must hope that by the help of divine grace he will persevere till the end in his holy resolutions.

Most powerful God, who upon our altars dost work so surprising a division, employ Thy word, that is Thy holy inspirations, as a two-edged sword, to separate my soul from all that may hinder its union with Thee; be Thyself all its support and all its strength; establish Thy abode in it for ever, so that possessing Thee, it may no longer need to lean upon any created thing.

This great miracle is followed by another equally prodigious: it is that the accidents of bread and wine, though separated from their substance, still do not fail to produce many effects, and that these are not merely proportioned to their natural virtue which is weak and imperfect, but they produce many others more noble which belong rather to substances than to accidents. It is indeed truly wonderful, that of themselves

[21] Is 28:20
[22] 1 Sam 5:3

they act with as much perfection as if they were still united with their substance; this is because divine power supplies for the substance which no longer exists; so much so that besides producing other accidents, such as odour, warmth and taste, they also nourish and fortify the body as if they were truly still bread and wine. In this we see the fulfilment of the Scripture: *Not alone in bread doth man live, but in every word that proceedeth out of the mouth of God;*[23] that is, by all that God wills shall serve him for nourishment. For here it is not at all by the bread that man lives, but by the hand of God Who, co-operating in a miraculous way with the accidents of bread, operates through them effects which are extraordinary and supernatural.

This shows us how just souls, detached from things of earth and sustained by grace, fortified besides by this heavenly food, not only acquit themselves as they ought of their ordinary duties and exercises, but undertake also great things above their natural strength, because then the omnipotence of the Creator supplies for the impotence of the creature. Of this we have notable examples in the martyrs who offered themselves to the most horrible torments, in the confessors and virgins, who have treated their bodies with inconceivable severity. Why then, weak and cowardly as we are, do we think that we could not live without bread, as if it were difficult for God to nourish with herbs and vegetables those who have been accustomed to eat only delicate meats? Why do we presume to set limits to His power, as if He could not make use of the weakest instruments to execute the greatest designs? Let everyone say boldly with St Paul: *I can do all things in Him who strengtheneth me*, by the power of this divine bread;[24] or with Job: *Set me beside Thee, Lord, and let any man's hand fight against me*,[25] for if Thou

---

[23] Deut 8:3, Mt 4:4
[24] Phil 4:3
[25] Job 17:3

art with me, if Thou comest to my aid, there is no difficulty that I cannot overcome. Most powerful God, who choosest the weak things *of the world to confound the strong… that no flesh may glory in Thy sight,*[26] show Thine infinite power by using me, the weakest of men, for the advancement of Thy glory and the confusion of Thy enemies.

III. Of the manner in which Christ our Lord is present in this Sacrament

The *fifth* miracle, which is indeed stupendous, is that the entire body of Christ our Lord, in all its integrity and beauty, as it is in Heaven, is present in this most holy Sacrament in a most singular manner. For it is present whole and entire in the Host and in every particle of the Host, as if it were pure spirit; just as our soul is whole and entire in our whole body and in every member of it. Hence it is that Christ our Lord under the sacramental species possesses true flesh, yet He does not live the life of the flesh with its functions and powers: He has hands and feet, but He does not walk or feel. He has a palate, yet He does not taste; He has a tongue, but He does not speak; He has eyes and ears, though here He makes no use of them: if He sees and hears, it is with the eyes of the spirit and the ears of the heart. Lastly, in this state to which He has reduced Himself, He is deprived of every pleasure which can enter the soul through the gate of the senses, as if He were altogether bereft of feeling.

These are the means which the divine omnipotence and wisdom have devised in order to prepare for true Christians a spiritual nourishment out of the flesh of the divine Lamb. Some of His disciples who were as yet gross and carnal held this doctrine in horror and even thought it to be impossible:

[26] 1 Cor 1:27-29

How, they said, *can this man give us His flesh to eat?... This saying is hard, and who can hear it?*[27] From that moment they abandoned their Master and walked no more with Him. Then Jesus, turning to those who were still at His side, and willing to reveal to them the whole truth, said to them: *It is the spirit that quickeneth: the flesh profiteth nothing.* My *words are spirit and life.*[28] As if He had said in plain terms: Do not take My words in a carnal sense, as have done those who have forsaken Me; My flesh shall not be eaten in the same manner as you would eat the flesh of animals: it shall be consumed after a spiritual manner, as if it were indeed a spirit which cannot be divided: because it is living flesh and will give life to those who eat it after this manner; for it shall change them from fleshly into spiritual.

In order that we may understand what that life is that we receive in this Sacrament, we have only to look at the Sacrament itself, in which it is clearly represented. Like other people, the just are composed of ordinary flesh and blood; but as soon as they have eaten this living bread, they begin to live a life so spiritual and so unlike that of the flesh that they can say with the Apostle: *Though we walk according to the flesh, we do not war according to the flesh.*[29] For in all that is opposed to the divine will, although we have eyes and ears, we see not, we hear not; we have a tongue and taste, yet we neither taste nor speak; we have hands and feet, but they do not serve us either for walking or acting. We renounce sensual pleasures as soon as God forbids them to us; we only think of what regards His service, and *by the Spirit,* as says St Paul, *we mortify the deeds of the flesh,*[30] in order to live a life perfect, spiritual and entirely conformed to that of Christ our Lord in the Holy Eucharist.

[27] Jn 6:53, 61
[28] *Ibid,* 64
[29] 2 Cor 10:3
[30] Rom 8:13

Upon this marvel follows another, not less stupendous. For although the sacramental species may be divided into many parts, yet the body and blood of Jesus Christ are not divided, but remain whole and entire in every particle, however small, because division is wont to be made in visible things, but invisible things and such as are spiritual, are indivisible. This may to some extent be illustrated by a homely example: when we look at ourselves in a mirror, we see the whole of ourselves; if we break the mirror, we can still see ourselves entire in each of the pieces, as we did before in the unbroken mirror. Hence it is that he who receives only a particle of a Host receives as much as one who receives a whole Host; and we receive Jesus Christ just as entire in a small Host as in a large one. Thus is every day renewed the miracle of the manna, of which it is written that *neither had he more that had gathered more: nor did he find less that had provided less,*[31] because all was reduced to a common measure.

Is not this a very accurate picture of that integrity of heart and interior recollection which can be obtained by virtue of this Sacrament? For although we are often obliged by our daily duties to attend to many things which may distract us, yet we must never suffer our heart to be divided[32] by many passions attaching it to creatures, for fear lest this division should cause our ruin. On the contrary, in the midst of the labours of Martha, we must preserve that *one thing* which Mary never lost;[33] our mind must always be recollected and united with our Creator; all the exercises of the active life must have for object the glory of God; our only intention should be to accomplish the divine good pleasure in great things as in little, even to the smallest details, setting before ourselves no other

[31] Ex 16:18
[32] Cf. Os 10:2
[33] Lk 10:43

aim or object, and doing everything in the spirit of our Lord. By this means we shall be always full of joy, equally content in poverty or in abundance, in lowliness or elevation; because all our happiness will be to fulfil what God wants of us: thus humiliation or honour will be all one to us, since we shall take either equally as the most dear will of God. Lastly, all those who aspire to the highest degree of prayer and contemplation may approach our Lord hidden in the Sacrament, in order to hide themselves from the eyes of the world, to recollect themselves with themselves, to close the doors of their senses, to let their spiritual powers alone act, to converse interiorly with God alone, to contemplate in deep repose His divine perfections, and to unite in Him, as in their centre, all their thoughts and all their desires, by virtue of this heavenly bread, which is the symbol of union and peace.

Bread of life, which conserves and joins together in Thine elect the active and contemplative lives, govern and rule so entirely all the motions of my heart that the cares of the one do not take from it the recollection and peace of the other. Wine that makes virgins, purify and set in order the affections of my heart in such fashion that I may only love my Creator in all His creatures. My God, hidden under the species of the Sacrament, *hide me* in Thy bosom and *in the secret of Thy face*[34] unite all my powers among themselves and with Thee, that I may think only of Thee, and love Thee alone. Amen.

IV. Of the coming of Christ our Lord into the Sacrament

The last of these miracles is that although Christ our Lord dwells always in highest Heaven and there enjoys the elevation which is His due, without leaving it, He yet descends on all the

[34] Ps 30:21

altars on which the holy Sacrifice of the Mass is offered, and thus is found at one and the same time in an infinite number of places, however poor, however abandoned they may be. His watchful providence, which never sleeps, is wonderfully exemplified in His prompt obedience to every priest who consecrates; for no sooner are the words of consecration said over the bread and wine in His name than He is present to make them good; so that immediately the priest has said: "this is My body", and "this is the chalice of My blood", He is here, as we have said above: *the Lord obeying the voice of a man,*[35] a priest, not only if he is in the state of grace and pronounces the words with a good intention, but even if he is in bad dispositions and says them with the intention of contemning Christ and communicating in mortal sin: Christ does this not only once a day but as often as they desire.

For the all-powerful God descends thus on our altars at every moment, and joins Himself in an admirable manner to the sacramental species for as long as they last, remaining in whatever place He is put, without showing any resentment either of the bad dispositions of such as receive Him unworthily, like Judas, nor the poverty of the place where He is kept, nor the outrages He receives from heretics, nor the blasphemies which are uttered against Him by the wicked. For just as He was obedient even to the death of the cross, persevering till His last breath, so for our sake He comes into the most holy Sacrament, in which He remains until the species of bread and wine are corrupted. And so He will remain with us even till the consummation of the world, according to His promise: *Behold, I am with you all days, even to the consummation of the world.*[36] Is not this a prodigious example of perfect obedience, invincible perseverance? Of virtues worthy to be imitated and admired by the whole world?

[35] Jos 10:14
[36] Mt 28:20

Consider attentively, my soul, these divine virtues, and endeavour to read them in that book of which we have spoken above, and to eat them, that thou mayest make them thine own. Henceforth, my Saviour, I hope to imitate Thy obedience, so humble and prompt: subjecting myself not only to my superiors, but to my inferiors, *not only to the good and gentle, but also to the froward*,[37] as Thou also didst. For I desire to renounce my own will absolutely, to do only the will of those who govern me in Thy place, performing what they enjoin so promptly and joyfully, with so inviolable a fidelity, that I shall choose rather to die than to fail in obedience. O Living Bread, O Bread which came down from Heaven, to bestow eternal life on those who eat Thee, since *my life* consists in *fulfilling Thy will*,[38] grant me grace ever to receive Thee with such dispositions that I shall ever esteem *my meat* to be to *do His will* who has bestowed on me such blessings.[39]

Here we have to remark a very marvellous thing, which greatly enhances the miracle; it lies in this, that although, to make good the words of consecration it would suffice that the body of Christ our Lord should be present entire under the accidents of bread, and His blood under the accidents of wine, He has willed none the less that both in the Host and in the chalice they should be present together, with all the other properties with which they are united, without one being absent. Whoever therefore receives the Host, receives the body, the blood, the soul of Jesus Christ and the Person of the Word with the divinity which subsists in the Word, by which He is so absolutely one with the Father and the Holy Spirit that these three Persons can never be separated one from the other. So also, whoever receives the chalice receives Jesus Christ entire, His body, His soul, His

---

[37] 1 Pt 2:18
[38] Ps 29:6
[39] Cf. Jn 4:34

divinity: hence it is that priests who communicate under both kinds receive no more than the laity who communicate under the species of bread alone, since both one and the other receive Jesus Christ whole and entire. Hence it is also that many prodigious effects which the Scripture attributes to the bread ought to be attributed to the wine also; as those which belong only to wine should be attributed reciprocally to the bread. For this reason it would be true to say that the bread quenches our thirst, that it inebriates, that it brings forth virgins, like the wine; in like manner, that the wine equally satisfies hunger, nourishes and fortifies, as if it were bread.

But in both the bread and the wine the Son of God makes us experience His infinite charity and liberality; for it is here, as says the prophet Aggaeus, that He *moves the heavens and the earth*,[40] that He works prodigious miracles, joining His body and His blood which come from Heaven, with bread and wine, which are produced by the earth, and thus every day fulfils that prophecy which brings *the desired of all nations* to His temple, which is His *house,* and which *He fills with His glory.* What charity could be more tender, what benevolence greater than that God should give us whatever He has of *good and beautiful,*[41] reversing the order of nature, that He may give us His grace.

God might very well have supplied for our spiritual nourishment by giving us blessed bread and wine, Christ our Lord from heaven using them as instruments to work those effects in our souls which He now produces through His body and blood: for the Son of God, without descending from His throne, could by simply blessing them communicate to them the power to produce the same effects which He operates by His own presence, just as in the other sacraments He uses pure water, oil, or balsam. But this did not suffice for His charity, infinite in its generosity,

[40] Agg 2:7
[41] Zach 9:17

for He is not content unless He Himself comes in person to provide for miserable sinners, wretched creatures, a magnificent banquet of His own body and blood, His soul and His divinity.

If a prince, while entertaining magnificently all the magnates of his kingdom, should call to mind a poor man, destitute of all help, covered with ulcers, lying on straw, dying of hunger in a hovel, and, touched with compassion, should send to him by one of his officers a dish from his own table, doubtless this action would be admired as a work of rare charity: if he were to command one of the greatest lords to rise from table and himself carry the dish to the unfortunate man, it would be a still more remarkable token of the love and esteem which he had for him; if the prince, rising from table himself, carried the dish, offering it to the beggar with his own hands, there is no one who would not be astounded at so great an excess of kindness; perhaps some would even ridicule it as an extravagance or as a condescension unworthy of the king's majesty.

O immense greatness! O infinite extent of the love of God for men! What an earthly prince would disdain to do, the King of heaven does every day in a manner so condescending that one could scarcely imagine it possible. This sovereign Ruler, as He said Himself,[42] is seated at His table with all the princes of His court, for whom He prepares a continual banquet, whom He regales and fully satisfies by the vision of His essence and His divine perfections: in the midst of this joyful feast, He remembers a poor man, who lies here below sick and half dead, in filth and infection, without a morsel of bread to stay the hunger which devours him. He has pity on him, He resolves to give him the remains of the royal banquet, that is, a share in the delights, the consolations and the holy joys which will be experienced eternally and without any weariness in Paradise. But these things He will not impart by the hands of the angels

[42] Cf. Lk 22:30

who serve Him, nor by the seraphim who guard His throne; He descends from heaven, He comes in person to visit him, though in an invisible manner, under the veil of the accidents of bread and wine; He makes Himself his nourishment and communicates to him His gifts, according to the dispositions in which He finds him.

If you do not know what it is to love, you will esteem all this folly, for, as St Bernard says,[43] it is like speaking Greek to a man who has never learned it, to talk of love to a man who has never loved. But if you have had some experience of it, you will easily believe what I have said about it, because one of the properties of love is to imagine a thousand ways of uniting oneself with the beloved, of sharing with them all one has, and of leaving no stone unturned to gain their love in return. Since then the wisdom and power of God are infinite, and His love is equally infinite: can you doubt that He has the knowledge, the power and the will to do everything which can be done to make us love Him as He desires?

Infinite Love, what shall I do that I may love Thee as Thou lovest me? Shall I not give all I have, even though it be very little? Since Thou bringest to me all Thou hast, which is so great? I will search out as many means of serving Thee as Thou hast found ways of enriching me with Thy gifts.

These, dearest brother, are seven inventions of divine love, on which thou oughtest to meditate frequently, together with those other seven of which we have spoken in chapter XII, saying with David: *I will meditate on all Thy works: and will be employed in Thy inventions,*[44] thanking Thy Saviour for all of them, in these words of Isaias: I *say to the just man that it is well, for he shall eat of the fruit of his doings.*[45]

---

[43] Serm. 79, *in Cant.*
[44] Ps 76:13
[45] Is 3:10

My Saviour, more just than all the just, and the Saint of saints *par excellence,* how happy and holy are all Thine inventions in our regard! Blessed be that wisdom which has searched them out, blessed be the power which has executed them, and the charity which has willed and chosen them. It is certain, Lord, that Thou dost eat of their fruits; for Thou dost draw to Thyself many souls who, meditating on these inventions, love Thee with a fervent and efficacious love, such as Thine own. For the fruit of Thy inventions is found in the Apostles, Martyrs, Virgins, Anchorites, and religious who desire to show a love for Thee corresponding to Thine for them; and now they eat and enjoy in Heaven the fruit of those inventions of love which they have shown on earth. Who will grant me to be united with these just souls, meditating so fervently on Thine inventions that I may love Thee with a love like Thine own; by which I also, like them, may eat the fruit of my inventions, enjoying Thee for all eternity! Amen.

Chapter VII

Of the love which unites us with Jesus Christ and with our neighbour, and which is an effect of the Sacrament of the Eucharist... of the different degrees of this union.

IN THE PRECEDING chapter we have sufficiently explained all that concerns the coming of our Lord into the Sacrament, the manner in which He unites Himself with the sacramental species and what He teaches us by this union, as well as the example He gives us of the most heroic virtues. Let us now see in what manner He comes into those souls who receive Him at the holy table and how He unites Himself with them, in order that having well considered the notable favours He bestows on them, we may endeavour to participate therein.

In the first place, we must suppose, with St Denis,[1] that love wheresoever we find it, whether in God, or in the angels or in men, has one virtue which is proper and essential to it, that is, to unite the one who loves to the object of his love. St Augustine[2] says that love is an invisible bond joining two friends together by an entire conformity of inclinations and feelings, as the Scripture testifies that "the soul of Jonathan was knit with the soul of David, and he loved him as his own soul."[3] The philosophers[4] were accustomed to say that those who loved one

---

[1] Lib. 4, *De divinis nominibus*
[2] Lib. 8, *De Trinit.,* cap. x. St Thomas Aquinas, Summa Theologiae, Ia-IIae, q. 28, a. 1, ad 2
[3] 1 Sam 18:1
[4] Aristophanes, *apud* Aristot., II Polit., cap. 2

another would desire, were it possible, to have but one body and one soul, and to be but one person: this Plato explained by a fable of two intimate friends who, meeting Vulcan one day, stood still. Vulcan asked them what they desired of him, and offered to do for them anything which belonged to his trade. The only thing we desire, they replied, is that you would plunge us both into your furnace, and that you would so soften us in it that, melted together, we might become but one man. This shows how much those who are animated by a mutual love desire to be united together and how many means love will suggest to satisfy this craving. But what is imaginary and impossible with men is both possible and true with God; for as He loves His creatures with an infinite love and is moreover omnipotent, He desires to unite Himself with them as much as He can and as is befitting His majesty. Therefore He does not content Himself with that common union which He has with all things by His essence, His presence and His power; nor with that closer union which He has with all just men in this life by His grace; nor even that which He has with the Blessed in Heaven by the light of glory: He has devised two others, entirely miraculous and beyond the comprehension of any created intellect.

The first is that of the divine Word with a human nature in Jesus Christ, at once true God and true man; Son of God by His eternal generation and Son of Mary by temporal generation. God has allied Himself with man, and by a wonderful device of His ever ingenious love He has contrived that of two natures He has formed one Jesus Christ, in such a way that the divine nature has relinquished none of its perfections nor has the human nature lost any of its natural qualities, as we have said elsewhere. Yet for all that, although the Word, as St Thomas observes,[5] by becoming man has enriched and ennobled all men, He has only

[5] *Opusc.* 58, cap. 5

honoured one single man with the hypostatic union, because it was not befitting His greatness to make that divine union too common. He has not even willed that all men should enjoy His visible presence: He showed Himself only to a small number of persons who were of His company, or who touched His garments, kissed His hands and feet, or put their fingers into His wounds; one Virgin alone, by a special privilege, had the honour of bearing Him for nine whole months in her womb. The divine wisdom has therefore sought out another kind of union which, after the first, is the most noble and perfect that could possibly be; it is that by which this God-Man, burning with love for men, communicates Himself indifferently to all, makes Himself their food and drink, places His sacred body under the accidents of bread, His precious blood under the accidents of wine; this He does in order that He may enter into each one of them, to unite them so intimately with Himself that they appear to be transformed into Him, and so to remain united with them as long as the sacramental species are unchanged, and during this time to heap upon them all the riches which a friend so liberal and so powerful can communicate to His friends.

These are the new and unheard-of things which the Prophet commands us to consider: he brings to our minds the mystery of the Incarnation which is continually renewed in the Holy Eucharist: *How long wilt thou be dissolute in deliciousness, O wandering daughter?* Remember that *the Lord hath created a new thing upon the earth; a woman shall compass a man.*[6] As if he said: Call to mind that the All-powerful, in order to fill you with His delights, has worked an incomparable miracle; He has enclosed Himself entire within the womb of a Virgin, and this Virgin bears a Man who, beneath the exterior of a child, hides the wisdom and the sanctity of a perfect man. But the marvel goes much farther than that: it will be perpetuated for

[6] Jer 31:22

all future centuries and will be renewed every day until the end of the world. For whosoever shall eat the bread of life shall receive into himself Jesus Christ, Who, under the sacramental species, has not only the sanctity and the wisdom but also the plenitude of the age of a full-grown man; he truly receives Him as He is in Heaven; every time that he has the happiness to receive Him he will taste ineffable delights, which will every time seem to him as new as if he had never tasted them before. O the depth of the treasures of wisdom, power and bounty of God! What other wisdom than a divine wisdom could have invented a thing so marvellous and so singular? What other power than an infinite power could have put it into execution? What bounty other than a bounty without limit could have used it as a means of enriching its friends and closely uniting itself with them?

Enlighten my eyes, Lord, with Thy wisdom; make me to understand the miracles of Thy omnipotence; enkindle me with the holy flames of Thy charity; receive me into Thy bosom, that I may come forth from that furnace as if melted and all transformed by love into Thine infinite bounty.

I. Of the spiritual union of the soul with Jesus Christ

This sacramental union has for its end and principal effect the spiritual union of the soul with its Saviour, and it is so strong that of two spirits it makes but one, so that St Paul was able to say that *he who is joined to the Lord is one spirit.*[7] So that those who eat the flesh of the Lord no longer live but by His spirit and are no longer, so to speak, but one spirit with Him; just as among created things there is nothing which so becomes one with a man as the food he takes, because it is converted

[7] 1 Cor 6:17

into his substance and communicates to him its own qualities. If his fare is delicate, the man's body becomes delicate, if it is coarse, he becomes robust: in like manner, when the Son of God gives Himself to the just as a food which nourishes them spiritually, He unites Himself most intimately with them.

But between this celestial food and common food there is a notable difference which the Lord Himself taught one day to St Augustine,[8] saying: '*I am the nourishment of grown men; grow and you shall eat me; nevertheless, you shall not change Me into yourself, but I shall change you into Myself.*' That is to say, he who eats common foods digests them and destroys them in order to change them into his own substance, and by destroying them in this fashion, he gives them a more noble being; he communicates to them his own life, and thus bears them about with him wherever he goes. On the contrary, he who eats this living bread is himself destroyed; he ceases to be what he was and begins to be what Jesus Christ is: it is Jesus Christ who is his life, it is He who forms, who rules all his thoughts, all his words, all his deeds; so that he may even say with St Paul: *I live, now not I; but Christ liveth in me.*[9] This great Apostle, as St Denis[10] remarks, lived like one who loves, who no longer lives in himself but in the object of his love. His only pleasure was to converse with his Saviour; he found no repose but in Him; he walked always in His presence; he strove, to the utmost of his power, to imitate His works; he forgot himself in order to think only of Jesus Christ.

It was with good reason that Plato used to say that the soul of a lover is dead in his own body and living in that of another. In truth, the soul which loves our Lord is as if dead and insensible to all that concerns its own interests; nothing has power

[8] St Augustine, Confessions, B. 7, ch. 10
[9] Gal 2:20
[10] See above

to touch it save the interests of Him whom it loves; it regards itself as a part of its Beloved, it lives in Him and for Him; and this, says St John Chrysostom,[11] is the essential character of those who love ardently. But who can express the excellence of this spiritual union with our Saviour? Who can understand the perfection of that life which it produces in holy souls? Christ our Lord, when He Himself desired to give us a high esteem of it, did not scruple to compare it to that eternal and incomprehensible union which He has always had with His Father: *Whoever,* He said, *eateth My flesh and drinketh My blood, abideth in Me and I in him: As the living Father hath sent Me and I live by the Father, so he that eateth Me, the same shall live by Me.*[12] What a miracle of divine charity is resplendent in this mystery of love! What closer degree of union could there be than that which deserves to be compared with the union of the Father with the Son? Nevertheless, it is true to say that as the Son by His eternal generation receives being, life and all perfections from the Father: so those who eat the flesh of the Saviour receive in proportion the being, life and virtues of the Saviour; they no longer have any other sentiments than His, any other will but His, and they make it all their glory to do what He has done. That is why St Gregory of Nyssa says that He who is, and who cannot cease to be what He is, makes Himself our nourishment, in order that, ceasing to be what we are, we may become what He is; what He is by nature, we become by grace.

Whenever then, we communicate worthily, we eat Jesus Christ and Jesus Christ eats our spirit and heart and transforms us entirely into Himself, just as we, when we take some nourishment, convert it into our own flesh and make it part of ourselves. These two things are pointed out to us by the Spouse of souls, who invites us to His banquet in these words: *I stand*

[11] St John Chrysostom, Hom. 61 *ad pop.,* et 41, *in Joan.*
[12] Jn 6:57

at the gate and knock: If any man shall hear My voice, and open to Me the door, I will come in to him, and will sup with him and he with Me.[13] That is to say, I will come, and I will enter into his heart; I will fill it with graces and we will eat together; he shall receive My body in the Sacrament, and from this tree of life he will pluck excellent fruit; for My part, I will receive his spirit, I will transform it into Mine in order that it may be no longer such as it was, but by a faithful and constant imitation, it shall become such as I am.

O Saint of saints, perfect model of the just! Blessed be Thou who hast deigned to make Thyself man and the food of man; I rejoice with Thee for the glory Thou hast deigned to derive from this: eat, O Lord, the hearts of them that eat Thee; transform them into Thyself, fill them with Thy spirit, that they may live no longer for themselves but for Thee alone; may they love Thee as Thou dost love them; dwell in them and make them to dwell in Thee for ever and ever. Amen.

II. Of the various degrees of this spiritual union

In order to conceive a higher esteem of this admirable union, it is well to notice its degrees and its effects, which differ according as those who communicate bring to this Sacrament dispositions more or less perfect.

The first degree of union with Christ our Lord is accomplished by means of sanctifying grace, which restores to the soul the life it had lost by sin. The Eucharist, which contains the most pure flesh of the divine Word, and which is the living bread, has such power that it effectively restores the life of grace to one who has lost it, if he communicates not knowing that he is in mortal sin or if he cannot find a confessor, and

[13] Apoc 3:20

believes himself to have made an act of perfect contrition. The efficacy of the sacraments of the New Law is specially shown in this, that they supply for any defect of contrition in one who receives them having made such preparation as he shall judge reasonable and fitting to receive them worthily.

But it belongs especially to this divine Sacrament, as says St Thomas,[14] to preserve that union and that life of grace which we have received in baptism or in the tribunal of penance. For bodily food, although it were as potent as manna itself, does not suffice to sustain a perpetual union of soul and body, nor hinder those who eat it from dying either by a sudden death by violence, or from disease or old age; *those* on the contrary *who eat this bread shall live for ever*[15] says the Saviour Himself, because if they so will, they shall never die the death of sin, and this bread, which the prophet calls the *wheat of the elect,*[16] shall give them sufficient strength to preserve for all eternity the life of grace and the intimate union which they have with the author of life.

O the depth of the divine wisdom, which has known how to join with a little bread the cause of our predestination and the germ of life eternal! If thou desirest to be of the number of the elect in heaven, eat often of this tree of life which is in the midst of the paradise of the Church militant, by whose virtue thou mayest come to eat also of that *tree of life which is in the paradise* of the Church triumphant[17] where thou shalt see clearly the eternal God, whom thou dost now receive in the Sacrament. O tree of life, Christ Jesus, preserve me from eternal death, conserve in me that grace which unites me with Thee, until I reach that blessed life in which I shall enjoy Thee in glory for ever.

---

[14] IIIa, q. 29, a.1
[15] Jn 6:59
[16] Zach 9:17
[17] *To him that overcometh I will give to eat of the tree of life which is in the paradise of my God.* Apoc. 2:7

The virtue of the Sacrament of the Eucharist goes even beyond what we have already said. For whenever we communicate our soul receives an increase of grace and a fresh degree of union with God, because the soul can always continue to grow, which is not possible to the body. This appears to be the reason why the Septuagint, inspired by God, calls this Sacrament the *bread of the young;*[18] for one of the properties of the Eucharist is to preserve in just souls a certain spiritual youth, so that they never grow old nor fall into relaxation and tepidity, being renewed like eagles[19] in ever greater fervour of spirit. Whosoever desires therefore, with holy Job, to *renew the days of his youth,*[20] and to live over again those *beautiful days when God was secretly in his tabernacle,* let him eat the bread of the elect; then this God who hides Himself under the visible species of the Sacrament will restore to him his youth, will pour into his soul the milk of heavenly consolation and make the oil of devotion flow abundantly in his heart: with this oil He will enlighten, heal, and strengthen him, and relieve all his pains.

If anyone asks me how this renovation of just souls is effected by Christ our Lord in this Sacrament, I answer that it is by exciting them to unite themselves to Him by ever fresh acts of love, drawing them after Him by His lights and divine inspirations, filling them with joy and fully satisfying them with His real presence. This is that spiritual refection proper to this divine Sacrament, since it is eminently the *cellar of wine* of the heavenly Spouse;[21] into which He introduces His friends. There it is, as says St Ambrose,[22] that He so inebriates them that, busying themselves no longer with the things of this world, losing

[18] *Frumentum juvenum*
[19] *Renovabitur ut aquilae juventus tua.* Ps 102:5
[20] Job 29:4
[21] Cant 2:4
[22] Serm. 15 on Psalm 118

even the fear of death, they forget all that might hold them to earth. The Eucharist is a hidden manna which, having in itself the source of all sweetness, seems so sweet to those who eat it that no one can imagine what it is like unless they have tasted it. It resembles the manna of the desert, which for the common people had but one taste, like to *that of flour with honey*,[23] but for the just had *in it all that is delicious and the sweetness of every taste*,[24] God desiring to regale and replenish them with the abundance of His sweetness. The Wise Man says again that it contained all that is most delicious in the choicest meats and that, *serving every man's will, it was turned to what every man liked*. Thus, although it was but a single substance, it seemed to be flesh, or fish, or fruit, or whatever a man desired to eat.

It is the same with this divine manna; it produces only ordinary grace and devotion in tepid souls who receive it with common dispositions: but it produces very great and very abundant fruit in those who partake of it with extraordinary fervour. It overwhelms them with joy, it excites in them various virtuous feelings according to their need and their desire: if they desire humility, it brings them humility; if they long for patience, it inspires them with patience; if they love the exercise of prayer and contemplation, it gives them the spirit of prayer and contemplation. For this Father, so merciful and liberal, who suits Himself to the will of those who fear Him, has no greater pleasure than to give them what they desire and what He knows will be profitable to them, according to the end for which He instituted this Sacrament; by this means He disposes them to accomplish His will more perfectly.

As then the Son of God, entering into the chaste womb of the Virgin,[25] filled her with such sweetness that she needed

[23] Ex 16:31
[24] Wis 16:21
[25] Lk 1:39-40

no other proof of His presence; and as, directly she had conceived, He urged her to start immediately for the mountain country of Judea, to the house of Zachary, where He desired to bestow wonderful marks of favour on His future Precursor, on Zachary himself and St Elizabeth: so, as soon as He enters into one who communicates fervently, He pours into his soul such marvellous spiritual joy as gives unmistakable proof of His presence. His heart becomes inflamed also with an ardent love of sanctity; He rouses in him an extreme impatience to attain the highest pitch of perfection and by the help of this divine guest to labour fruitfully for the salvation of souls.

O most merciful Guest, who dost deign to accommodate Thyself to the will of Thy children, in order that they may conform themselves to Thine, which conformity is *life and eternal salvation*:[26] help me to do Thy will on earth as it is done in Heaven; make me worthy to eat of this *daily bread*, that I may participate as far as is possible on this miserable earth in the happiness which the saints enjoy in the land of the living. *And since Thy delights are to be with the children of men*,[27] come and visit this son of man to make of him a child of God; and instead of the miseries with which he is filled, replenish him with Thy benedictions and heavenly delights.

This spiritual refection in which the soul is nourished by God is followed by another in which, after its own fashion, the flesh also tastes the fruit of the Sacrament. As soon as it is united to the body of our Lord, it becomes obedient to the spirit; its passions, says St Cyril,[28] begin to be obedient to reason, and the torrent of spiritual delights with which it is inundated causes it to abhor sensual pleasures. Hence it is that in the Scriptures

---

[26] *Et vita in voluntate ejus* Ps 29:6
[27] Prov 8:31
[28] Lib. 4, *in Joan.*, ch. 29

the Holy Eucharist is called *a wine springing forth virgins;*[29] for the most pure body of Christ makes all those who come in contact with it chaste. Although it has this property in the Host as much as in the chalice, it is attributed to it specially under the species of wine, in such sort that even from wine, which usually is only the cause of shameful passions,[30] our omnipotent Saviour generates virginity, because by enkindling us with His love He inebriates us after a fashion which extinguishes in us all the fire of self-love; all that which formerly served the devil as matter for temptation our Lord now makes use of to help us to conquer his seductions.

And since all the works of God are accomplished perfectly, this wine does not bring forth *foolish virgins* but *wise,*[31] virgins who are pure both in body and soul, virgins who are humble and charitable, who are not puffed up on account of their virginity, and who have always *in their lamps,* that is, in their hearts, *the oil* of charity, in order to *follow the Lamb whithersoever he goeth.*[32] Hence it is that it engenders not only virgins, but also martyrs, doctors, zealous preachers, excellent priests, holy religious, perfect men in every walk of life, valiant soldiers who, in frail and mortal flesh, do not fear to give battle to the prince of this world. True Christians, as says St John Chrysostom,[33] rise from this table like very lions, casting fire from their mouths and terrifying the demons. What wonder if, having within themselves the Lion of the tribe of Judah who has vanquished the ancient serpent, they become strong and generous as lions! Need we be astonished if, being filled with a devouring fire, they cast flames from their mouths and eyes?

---

[29] Zach 9:17
[30] *Et nolite inebriari vino, in quo est luxuria.* Eph 5:18
[31] Mt 25:2
[32] Apoc 14:4
[33] Hom. 16, *ad Pop.*

Whoever does not desire to be overcome ought to arm and fortify himself with the grace of this Sacrament, without which, as St Cyprian bears witness,[34] no one in the first centuries was permitted to expose himself to martyrdom, for fear lest if he were not sustained and fortified with this heavenly food he should succumb to the torment.

Most potent wine, producing the flowers of virginity and martyrdom, inebriate my heart with the strength of Thy love, that I may be able to overcome all the infernal powers and govern and rule all the desires of my own flesh. Bread of the elect, cooked under the ashes of humanity and charity, Who art also the sword of Gedeon for the destruction of the armies of Hell,[35] strengthen me by Thy power, that I may overthrow them all; but to Thee be all the glory of my victory.

III. Of the love which unites us with our neighbour

From that love which unites just souls with Christ our Lord in the Eucharist is born the charity which unites them all among themselves; for, according to the axiom of the philosophers, when two things are united with a third, they are also united with each other, as we see that two arms, being joined to one body, have between themselves a mutual union and correspondence. Since then, just persons who communicate with the necessary dispositions are united spiritually with Jesus Christ, they are united also with one another; they tend all to have the same thoughts, desires, inclinations and works, conformed to those of Jesus Christ, by Whom they live;[36] they will acquire patience and humility like to His; with Him they

---

[34] Epist. 14
[35] Judges 7:13-14
[36] Jn 6:58

will practise all virtues; and this is indeed one of the principal effects of the Eucharist, as says St Paul: *We, being many, are one bread, one body, all that partake of one bread.*[37] In these few words the Apostle admirably explains the excellence of the union of souls among themselves through their union with the Saviour in the Eucharist, on what it is founded, in what manner it is brought about, and what are the fruits we may gather from it.

For in the first place, when he says that all who eat this heavenly food are one bread, what does he mean but that they imitate so perfectly the King of all virtue and attach themselves so closely to Him, only forming, so to speak, with Him but one living bread, that they begin to live only by His spirit? For indeed, as all the Hosts in the world are truly but the same living bread, which is Jesus Christ, although the sacramental species are many; so all those who communicate worthily receive the spirit of Jesus Christ Who lives in them, and Who makes them live with the same life as Himself, although they are many persons. Still more, as all the Hosts which are consecrated lose their own substance to receive that of Christ our Lord, which is common to them all, so those who eat as they should the body of the Saviour, retain nothing of their own spirit; they are no longer led but by the Spirit of the Saviour; they renounce their own judgement and their own will; they combat their natural inclinations which are a cause to them of trouble and interior strife; they follow no other motives than those by which the Spirit of Christ guides them; and being all united with Him in the bond of charity, they all have also among themselves the same sentiments, they act in concert as if they were many bodies which were animated by one single soul. In this they resemble the first Christians of whom it was said that *the multitude of the believers had but one heart and one soul.*[38] For if it is true that this divine bread is not converted

[37] 1 Cor 10:17
[38] Acts 4:32

into those who receive it, but on the contrary changes them into itself; it follows clearly that as soon as they have partaken of it, they find themselves transformed into the Spirit of Christ and all become one bread by conformity with this same Lord, who so transmutes them and changes them into Himself that they can all say with one voice those words of the Apostle: *I live, now not I; but Christ liveth in me.*[39]

Most sweet Christ, be Thou our sole Spirit; that all our spirits, as they are all united with Thine, may equally be united among themselves. Amen.

The manner in which the Eucharist unites the hearts of the faithful is again expressed in another fashion in these words: *We are all one bread.*[40] For, as remarks St Cyprian,[41] Christ our Lord chose for the matter of the Sacrament of His body a substance which is one, but composed of many things joined and mingled together. The bread is composed of many grains of wheat, the wine of many grapes, to mark that union of charity which this bread of angels operates among men, and which is admirably represented in the ear of corn and the cluster of grapes. The grains of corn and the grapes have between themselves two kinds of union, the one natural, the other artificial: the former consists in the natural arrangement by which the grains are associated together in one ear, the grapes in one cluster, and in which they greatly resemble one another in size, shape, taste and smell: the latter union, by destroying the former, augments and perfects it; for after the wheat or the grapes have been harvested, they are pressed, crushed and divided, the smaller from the greater, the better from the worse; from the more perfect is made the bread or the wine. But when the bread and the wine are made, when all the particles are mingled

[39] Gal. 2:20
[40] 1 Cor 10:17
[41] Epist. 63. Cf. St August., Tract. 26 on John

together, one can no longer discern the small from the large nor the black from the white, because they all together compose the same bread or the same wine; it is only necessary that the bread, to be cooked and fit for eating, should be subjected to the warmth of fire, and that the wine, to be fit for drinking, should purge itself by its natural heat from all impurity.

We see here an illustration of what happens to men also in this life: they are bound together both by nature and by grace. The first of these links comes from a common nationality, blood-relationship, the same profession, or a resemblance of natural temperament: from this proceeds that natural love by which parents love their children, and brothers, or neighbours, those whose likes and dislikes are akin, have some sort of affection or attachment for one another. But such kinds of friendship are of themselves very low and unworthy of a Christian soul; they are founded entirely on human considerations, and are earthly and terrestrial; in order to render them holy we must sift out all that is too natural, all that hinders divine grace from forming other intimacies at once more noble and more perfect. For which reason Christ our Lord Himself said that He came upon earth *not to send peace but the sword. For I came to set a man at variance with his father, and the daughter against her mother… and a man's enemies shall be those of his own household,*[42] just as when one separates the grains of wheat or the grapes from the bunch. In this way He makes of them a spiritual bread and wine; He rejects all that savours of earth; He destroys in them all affections inspired merely by flesh and blood; He banishes from their hearts all inordinate desires for the goods of this world, for honours, pleasure and so forth, which frequently injure the union which we ought to have with our neighbour. For when they are thus disengaged from all temporal interests, they begin to be truly united among

[42] Mt 10:34-36

themselves, they become but one thing by the fire of charity, warmth of devotion, or fervour of spirit, and so they are more and more united together until they can say with the Apostle: *We are but one bread, we who all eat of the same bread, who participate in the same chalice.*[43]

As soon, then, as our Lord comes into those who receive Him at the holy table, the first thing that He does is to take from them all that may hinder this union of charity: He urges them powerfully to become detached from their relatives, friends, riches, empty honours and sensual pleasures; to divest themselves of all that is fleshly and of this earth, that they may live in peace and perfect concord with their neighbour. Sometimes He moves them to relinquish all these things in affection only; sometimes effectually and in very deed, as is done by religious, in order that this union may be closer, more excellent and more lasting; in this way are they truly made one bread, and we can no longer distinguish among them the great from the little, nor the free man from the slave,[44] since they are all, as it were, but one man, and the love they bear one another makes them all one in Christ Jesus. And finally, we shall see that accomplished which was foretold by the prophet Isaias, that one day *the wolf shall dwell with the lamb... and the lion shall eat straw like the ox;*[45] that is to say, that the great shall become as humble as the little; they will be ready to undertake the lowliest offices; they will abhor pre-eminence and distinctions; those who are of different humours and dispositions will ignore their natural antipathies, so that all will live in peace because the same Spirit of Christ dwells in them all.

Bread of life, what thanks and praise shall I return to Thee for this sweet and abiding union which Thou preservest among

[43] 1 Cor 10:17
[44] Cf. Gal 3:28
[45] Is. 11:6

us? Would to God that all the faithful might receive Thee with such holy dispositions that they might become one bread, a bread living and wholly spiritual! Would to God that they might be wholly transformed into Thee, and that they might begin to live a life like to Thine own!

This union of charity which binds us so closely one to the other, and which also makes us all equal, is not contrary, nevertheless, to a certain distinction necessitated by difference of rank and of employment. So St Paul says that we are not only one bread but also one body whose various members, although their functions are quite different, act in perfect harmony. For one of the effects of the Sacrament of the altar is to unite so closely together those whom God calls to different ministries in the mystical body or Church, or in a community, that this diversity causes no discord; the great cannot do without the little, nor do the little rebel against the great; all live in peace because all live by the same spirit; in this they resemble the members of the natural body which, having but one soul, all their functions are directed towards the same end, the good of the whole.

But the union which God desires us to cherish between ourselves, of whatever rank or condition we be, is again exemplified for us by the wonderful manner in which food is united to him who eats it; for it penetrates every part of the body and so takes to itself its nature and qualities that in the flesh it becomes flesh, in the bones it becomes bone. It is the same with those who communicate worthily: the fruit of their communion is that they accommodate themselves to the inclinations and needs of their neighbour in all that is conformable to the law of God, and which may serve to maintain peace in the world. They imitate the great Apostle who said: *I became all things to all men, that I might save all.*[46] I am sad with those

---

[46] 1 Cor 9:22; Rom. 12:15

in affliction; I rejoice with those who are glad; with the weak I am weak, little with the little, that I may be all things to them all by charity.

Divine Bread, by which the faithful are joined together on earth, as the Blessed are in heaven, communicate to all those who receive Thee that life which Thou dost possess and which Thou canst not lose, that being united with Thee, they may be so also among themselves for ever and ever, to the glory of Thy holy name. Amen.

IV. Of frequent Communion

We have now sufficiently explained the excellence and utility of the Sacrament of the altar; those who best know and appreciate its fruits are those who partake of it often. For though there is nothing in the whole world more precious and more excellent, there is nothing which can be obtained more easily, and this is not one of the least of its advantages. Those gifts which are bestowed by the liberality of princes, if they are of great price, are rarely given; if they are dealt out more frequently they are not of great price, because kings, however rich and powerful they may be, are not possessed of inexhaustible treasures. If they give much, they do not give often; if they give often the gift is of little value; because if they give both often and much, they would soon not be in a position to be able to give at all. Both these advantages are to be found in an eminent degree in this Sacrament, which is the gift of God Himself: for what is there greater or more extraordinary in the whole world than Jesus Christ, God and man? Nor is there anything more common than bread and wine, under whose accidents He hides Himself in order that we may be emboldened to receive Him frequently, giving Him infinite thanks for so precious a gift so frequently bestowed. For He is always at our beck and call, and never wearies of giving us His whole self, and all that He has.

The Israelites counted it a great favour that God should give them daily manna from Heaven;[47] nevertheless, He only nourished them with this miraculous bread for the space of forty years, while He has given us His flesh to eat for more than fifteen hundred years, and will continue to give it till the end of the world. The manna was only gathered in the morning; Jesus offers Himself to be our guest at all times, morning or evening, at any hour of the day or night is He ready to visit us. He says to us continually what He said to His Apostles: *I go away and I come unto you;*[48] I come from Heaven into this Sacrament for you that I may draw your soul back to Heaven with Me; I come and return again and again, nor will I give over until I have conducted you, soul and body, thither and made you to sit with Me on the throne of My glory. Knowing therefore how much this Lord desires to communicate Himself to us for our interest, not His own, shall we not endeavour to render ourselves worthy to receive Him often, not for our own profit, but to give Him the satisfaction He so ardently desires? Let us live so holily that we may at any time be ready to communicate worthily, and let our whole life be nothing but a continual and very perfect preparation for Holy Communion. By this means, our esteem for this adorable Sacrament will not be diminished by frequent reception; rather will it be augmented and we shall reap more abundant fruit.

Let us call to mind that among the seven petitions contained in the prayer taught to us by our Lord Himself, the fourth is for this heavenly bread, which is here called *daily* to teach us that we ought to show a great desire to eat it every day, and neglect

[47] Ex 16:35 (But now we may say: "over two thousand years". *N.E.*)
[48] Jn 14:28

nothing in order to partake of it with suitable dispositions. But notice that this petition is placed in the midst of the others because Holy Communion is the general means for obtaining all sorts of graces: if anyone aspires to the highest degree of perfection proper to the unitive life, the surest and shortest way to attain it is to approach frequently and with fervour to this holy table, where the Author of all perfection and sanctity Himself comes to us and where He pours out most liberally His gifts into our souls according to His perfect knowledge of our needs. St Laurence Justinian says[49] that love is like fire which in its own sphere burns continually and nourishes itself: but out of it is extinguished as soon as the wood is wanting.[50] Thus the priests of the ancient law were commanded to furnish wood every day for the altar, for fear lest the sacred fire should ever be extinguished;[51] and the Wise Man says that *as the wood of the forest is, so the fire burneth.*[52] The love of God, in the paradise which is its natural home, has no need for new benefits to sustain it; the clear vision of the Deity suffices, because it removes all that can stifle it or diminish its ardour; but here below, where it is out of its sphere, where on all sides it has enemies to combat and opposition to surmount, it would not subsist long if it were deprived of two things which contribute powerfully towards keeping it alight.

The first and chiefest of these is that some new benefit is never wanting to it on the part of Jesus Christ, our great Highpriest. For this Sovereign Pontiff desires that the sacred mysteries should be celebrated every day, in order that He may Himself come to cast wood on this fire, and that every time He comes He may increase His gifts and graces. Therefore He desires that all the faithful should actually receive Him daily, if

---

[49] *Serm. de Euchar*
[50] *Cum defecerint ligna, statim extinguitur ignis.* Prov 26:20
[51] Lev 6:12
[52] Ecc 28:12

on their part they have the necessary dispositions. The second thing which serves as fuel for this divine fire is the consideration of the motives capable of arousing the love of God in our hearts: this depends upon ourselves, as spiritual priests bringing daily wood for the fire in our meditations: wherefore we should dispose ourselves daily to make at least a spiritual communion, desiring if possible to receive Him sacramentally and preparing ourselves by fervent prayers and desires, humbly beseeching our Lord to heap spiritual wood on this fire, since His power is not confined to the Sacrament alone.

Most sweet Jesus, Who from Thy sacramental throne dost cry out: *I am come to cast fire upon the earth: and what will I, but that it be kindled?*[53] Come into the earth of my heart and kindle in it the fire of Thy divine love, feeding its flames with Thy presence so that it may burn continually. Immense God, *whose fire is in Sion, and His furnace in Jerusalem,*[54] for Thou dost remain in Thy Church in this Sacrament as in a furnace, emitting flames of heavenly love: set my cold heart on fire, that it may love Thee fervently in the holy Sion of the Church militant, until I enjoy Thee for ever in the Jerusalem of the Church triumphant. Amen.

Note. In reading the following chapter, it will doubtless be kept in mind that De Ponte was writing in an age when frequent, and still more daily, Communion was rarely permitted to the laity. One may easily deduce (especially from some of the prayers in the Appendix) with what delight so great a lover of the Blessed Sacrament would have welcomed the Decree of Pope St Pius X on Frequent and Daily Communion had it been promulgated in his lifetime. (Translator)

---

[53] Lk 12:9
[54] Is 31:9

Chapter VIII

That to the meditation of the mysteries of our Saviour ought to be joined mortification and imitation: in these three actions consists that spiritual communion which best disposes the soul for sacramental Communion.

IT NOW REMAINS to show with what dispositions we ought to approach the Sacrament of the altar if we wish to obtain that divine and spiritual union which is the principal fruit of this adorable Sacrament; but at the same time we ought to know by what the meditation of these mysteries should be accompanied.

To understand this well we must first remark that Christ our Lord in that solemn discourse in which He gave promise of this Sacrament joined together three kinds of eating, all of them truly mystical. The first is corporal and sensible; this He expressed, saying: *I am the bread of life: he that cometh to Me shall not hunger: and he that believeth in Me shall never thirst.*[1] The second is sacramental, in which under the accidents of bread and wine He is truly received, of which He said: he that eateth My flesh and drinketh My blood hath everlasting life.[2] Hereby He shows us that the first is a disposition to the second, and the second to the third, which perfects the other two, and of which we shall speak later. As then, three things must be done in order to nourish the body with food, first eating the meat, then digesting it by natural warmth, and lastly, having

[1] Jn 6:35
[2] *Ibid*, 55

digested and changed it into blood, converting it into our own substance; so also must we practise three things in order to nourish the soul, that is, meditation, mortification and imitation, from which proceeds resemblance. All these three were indicated by the Holy Spirit, saying by the mouth of Solomon:[3] *When thou shalt sit to eat with a prince, consider diligently what is set before thy face: and put a knife to thy throat, if it be so that thou have thy soul in thy own power. Be not desirous of his meats, in which is the bread of deceit.* St Ambrose and St Augustine both apply these words to the Holy Eucharist, following the Septuagint version, in which we read: *When thou art seated at the table of a powerful prince, take special note of what viands are set before thee: eat of them, but remember that thou shouldst serve him with the like.*[4]

Who is this great prince who invites us to his table if not Jesus Christ, the Prince of Peace, powerful in word and work?[5] What is this table, if not the Holy Scriptures, which contain for us the mysteries of our faith, or the Holy Eucharist, which is an excellent abridgement of them? To this table does He invite us, when He inspires us to read, or pray, or communicate. Let us remember that we ought not then to eat alone, but with this most wonderful Prince, who will observe all we do, who will teach us to do nothing but what is good, who will take pleasure in listening to us, and will converse familiarly with us. But it is not without mystery that He wills us to be seated, not standing, at his table: this is to show that we ought not to take our leave too soon, but remain until we have fully satisfied our hunger.

---

[3] Prov 23:1

[4] *Si sederis coenare ad mensam potentis, considerans intellige quae apponuntur tibi: et sic mitte manum tuam, sciens quod te talia oportet praeparare.*

[5] Lk 24:19

I. Of consideration

The first act of our spiritual eating is the consideration and meditation of those things *that are set before us;* which ought to be diligent and without distractions, attentive without sleepiness, and so profound as to penetrate to the very depths all that *is set before us.* For the table of the Lord, as St Bernard has well said,[6] resembles in a certain sense that of an earthly king, on which are set two sorts of objects, some intended to refresh the guests, such as delicious meats and choice wines; the others serve to manifest the greatness and magnificence of the prince, such as vessels of gold and silver. At such superb banquets a man would pass for uncivil who would not taste of the dishes offered him; but one who carried away the plate and ornaments would be reckoned a thief; the same reproach would be addressed to him as that which Joseph made to his brethren when, by a studied artifice, he accused them of having stolen his cup.[7]

The same two things appear in the Holy Scripture and in the Sacrament of the altar: these are two magnificently appointed tables on which we may find two sorts of objects, that is, virtues and miracles. Both of these merit our serious consideration: but we should remark that virtues are like the viands which nourish the soul, and of which we become worthy to partake by faithful and constant imitation, while miracles resemble the vessels of gold and silver. The object of these is to display the power and magnificence of God, although they serve also to satisfy and content the mind which considers them and fill it with admiration; while they increase the splendour of the virtues, they excite the will to love and practise them with greater earnestness. Nevertheless, it would be presumption and temerity to wish to work miracles, since

[6] *Serm. de Nativ., de S. Andrea, de S. Martino,* et alibi
[7] Cf. Gen 44:5

our Saviour Christ has not said *Learn of Me* to raise the dead, to give sight to the blind, but to be *meek and humble of heart*.[8] The virtues themselves, especially those which are exterior, are not equally suitable to all; this is why we ought to have a special affection for those of which we have most need, which we like best and which are most adapted to help us to perform our duties. To such as these also we ought principally to apply ourselves as those from which we may draw most profit; because the best dishes are neither so agreeable nor so wholesome when they are eaten with haste as when we masticate them at leisure.

Hence it is that the Holy Spirit[9] compares the throat of the Spouse to a super-excellent wine, worthy to be offered to the Beloved in order that He may drink it little by little and enjoy its flavour. By this He would teach us that the contemplative ought to employ much time on the consideration of the mysteries and virtues of Christ our Lord, the loving Spouse of our souls; because these mysteries and virtues are like delicious wines which He offers to His friends to drink, but in such fashion that they give themselves time to enjoy their flavour to the full. And lest any should think that this grace is only granted to the fervent, there is another version which reads that this wine touches the lips of the old;[10] by this is meant that as wine is necessary to the old to strengthen them, to hearten them, since old age makes them weak, cold, and sad; so those who have lost all the vigour, all the fire, all the lightheartedness of their spiritual youth ought to drink of this heavenly wine, which gives strength to those who are feeble, fervour to those who are tepid, and joy to those who are sad. Let us then do as the Holy Spirit counsels us: when we are at the table of the King of kings, let us pay attention to what is set before us; let

[8] Mt 11:29
[9] 'Thy throat is like the best wine.' Cant 7:9
[10] *Commovens labia senum.* See Titelman.

us clearly distinguish the virtues from the miracles; let us glorify the omnipotence and the bounty of the Lord who works these miracles, and to miracles joins such admirable virtues: let us admire and imitate those which He works in the mystery set before us, and in general all those which shine forth in Him; but let us attach ourselves especially to those which He proposes to us as most suitable to our state, and on which our perfection principally depends.

II. *Of mortification*

The second disposition necessary to communicate profitably is mortification; this is why the Holy Spirit desires that after we have considered what we ought to eat at the table of the prince, we should *put a knife to (our) throat*.[11] What is meant by this knife which we are to put to our throat, in which are situated the organs of speech and taste? It is a figure of mortification and discretion, because it will not suffice to meditate on the truths of faith if we have not these two virtues by which to crucify in ourselves the old man, to repress the daintiness of our taste, the intemperance of the tongue, and all which serve to feed the corruption of the flesh: it is impossible otherwise to know well and imitate as we ought the virtues of the Son of God. For just as meat cannot be converted into the substance of the body until it has been digested; so when the mind has penetrated the truths which are the subject of our meditation, it is necessary to place them before the will, that by the warmth of devotion it may change them into a wholesome spiritual aliment. Now the fruit of all this is an entire abnegation of self and a generous mortification, without which we shall never obtain the happiness of resembling Jesus Christ. Therefore He

[11] Prov 23:2

said one day to His disciples that *if anyone would come after Him, let him deny himself, and to take up his cross and follow Him.*[12] By this He would show that abnegation is the way which leads to imitation, and that by this road we reach the height of sanctity.

It is related by St Dorotheus that a certain abbot used to say: Give of your blood and you shall receive the Spirit of God;[13] because the gifts of the Holy Ghost are the reward of perfect mortification. What suffering should we not willingly submit to, even to shedding all our blood, if necessary, to overcome the wicked spirit and triumph over sin? Nothing will seem too difficult if we consider that the life of our Saviour was nothing but a continual succession of labours and sufferings; though His blood was so precious, He did not hesitate to pour it all out; His holy life was not too much to give for the salvation of His enemies. His soul was continually pierced by the sword of sorrow, and it was against Him that His Father had spoken this sentence: *Awake, O sword, against My Shepherd, and against the man that cleaveth unto Me.*[14]

Shepherd of souls, Man forever united to God, stimulate me by Thy example to practise a rigorous mortification, that being dead to the world I may live only for Thee and in Thee, without ever being separated from Thy divine Presence.

When we read that, being seated at the table of the prince, we should take a knife and put it to our throat, this is to teach us that in the exercise of prayer, during those happy moments when we taste most fully heavenly delights, when God Himself communes familiarly with us, we must not even then forget mortification. It is to our interest to watch at such times over the movements of our heart; not to let ourselves be carried away by transports of immoderate joy; not to feed our self-love

---

[12] Mt 16:24
[13] *Da sanguinem et accipe spiritum.* Serm. 10
[14] Zach 13:7

on a too great abundance of spiritual delights. Let us always be more keen to acquire solid virtue than to enjoy passing consolations; to put a bridle on our tongue and not to speak too much or with too little restraint before the Prince who has invited us to His banquet; to carry ourselves in His presence as if someone were holding a knife to our throat, ready to stab us, that is to say, trembling with fear lest we should be treated like that unhappy man who was chased shamefully out of the banquet-hall because he had come in without a wedding garment. As soon then as we dispose ourselves to prayer or approach the holy table, let us think that *now the axe is laid to the root of the trees,*[15] that the sword of divine justice is already drawn, that today will be perhaps the last of our life and that death is already near; doubtless such considerations will aid not a little, if well meditated, worthily to receive the body of the Lord. For in this action it is of extreme importance to join fear to love, in order to temper love by fear and fear by love. Without this we should never have the courage to take the knife in hand to sacrifice to God our animal and corporal life. Nevertheless, the Holy Spirit adds these remarkable words: *if it be so that thou have thy soul in thy own power,*[16] to show that we ought to have such command over all the powers of our soul that nothing shall oppose itself to reason, and that we should always be ready rather to lose our life than the grace of God.

III. Of imitation

The third disposition required by the Sacrament of the Eucharist is imitation of those virtues which we admire and love in the Son of God. In the first place we should make acts

[15] Mt 3:10
[16] Prov 23:1

of them in our heart, at the same time determining to practise them before men when occasion arises, according to the model we have set before us. For just as nourishment well digested and transformed into blood is distributed through all the veins, changed into the substance of the body, and united to the soul, which give the body its life, so the truths of the Gospel, searched out and penetrated, with the resolutions they inspire of mortifying ourselves, extend to all the virtues, to humility, to patience, to obedience and all the rest which, being joined together by the Spirit of God, become like the members of a body: they excite and aid each other to perform their several acts, they dispose the soul to receive the Holy Spirit who produces by them living works agreeable to the divine Majesty.

For this reason St Bernard says[17] that in our prayer, God gives us to drink of a spiritual wine which inebriates us and makes us forget the delights of the flesh, which penetrates to the very depths of the soul, which gives fervour for good works, sustains the interior powers, strengthens faith, fortifies hope and sets *charity in order,*[18] in one word, perfects in the soul whatever it there finds that is good. This is perhaps why the celestial Spouse, speaking of a mysterious wine of which his friends should taste, says, according to the Hebrew text, that when it enters into those who drink of it, it sets right all that is in disorder,[19] and puts all their powers and virtues into the right path, so that they may go straight to their goal without turning aside. From this we may gather the difference there is between this spiritual wine and the common sort: the latter makes what is straight to bend, the former sets upright what was not so; the latter disquiets the senses, the former clears

---

[17] Serm. 18, *in Cant.*
[18] Cant 7:9
[19] *Vadens dilecto meo in rectitudines;* or; *Vadens ad dilectum meum directe.* See Titelman.

them; the one causes us to speak much and without reserve, the other so restrains the tongue that we speak little and with discretion; finally, the one upsets everything while the other regulates all things so well that our own judgement gives way to that of others, our self-will subjects itself to the will of God, our appetites yield to reason, the movements of the exterior man are conformed to those of the inner, and both these take for their norm of conduct the new man, Jesus Christ, whom all ought to imitate.

We may pause here to reflect on what is added by the Holy Spirit, that when we eat at the table of a great prince, we should well consider the viands that are served, *because He expects that we should serve Him again with the like.*[20] Gratitude and justice alike demand that we should in our turn invite Him who has invited us and treat Him, if possible, with as much magnificence as He has treated us. Jesus Christ has done us the honour to invite us to His table; besides His adorable flesh and blood, He sets before us other exquisite meats: such are the examples He gives us of humility, obedience, charity and all other virtues. In order therefore that we may entertain Him in like manner, we must offer Him various acts of these same virtues; this is what is most to His taste, this He likes, this He asks of us when we communicate. Does He not assure us of this when He says in the Apocalypse that *if any man open to Me the door, I will come in to him, and will sup with him and he with Me?*[21] The repast with which He will regale us will be composed of graces, delights and heavenly consolations, with which He is wont to fill those who meditate upon His glories: the meal which we shall set before Him will be of ardent desires, fervent resolutions of serving Him, and other like sentiments which the enjoyment of His presence will excite in us. He will speak

[20] Prov 23:1 (Septuagint). See above.
[21] Apoc 3:20

and we shall answer Him; and as it will be our pleasure to listen to what He will say to us, so also will He delight to hearken to what we shall say to Him, whether we offer Him vows, whether we pray, or whether we return Him thanks and praise.

Here we have a full repast for the spirit, something that will completely satisfy the soul, for meditation alone does not suffice without mortification and imitation. Discourse and dry reasoning are like those aliments on which we sometimes feed in our dreams, imaginary food which pleases without nourishing, of which Isaias says:[22] *as he that is hungry dreameth, and eateth, but when he is awake, his soul is empty.* And indeed, it is only too common that after long and vain speculations we feel in ourselves no greater strength, courage and fervour than before; the reason is that we have not partaken of the true nourishment of the soul, that nourishment to which the Son of God alluded when He said: *My meat is to do the will of Him that sent Me, that I may perfect His work;*[23] as if He would say: that on which I live and feed is not the knowledge of My Father's will, but the accomplishment of it; it is not simply to renounce My own will but to renounce it in order to obey Him who sent Me, to be ready ever to execute His orders promptly and faithfully, and neither to will nor to do anything but what pleases Him.

O my most sweet Saviour, ever give me this nourishment that by it my spirit may be continually sustained and fortified, that my mind may be fed upon the bread of meditation, that my will may eat the bread of mortification, that my whole soul may be nourished by the bread of imitation; do Thou also feed on that bread which so delights Thee, that namely of seeing Thy servant joyfully accomplish all that Thou dost command him.

[22] Is 29:8
[23] Jn 4:34

IV. Of preparation for Communion

It is clear, and by this time my readers ought to be fully persuaded, that the best preparation for sacramental Communion consists in the three things of which we have just spoken. In the first place then, we must consider, according to what has been said, the excellence of the Sacrament of the Eucharist in order to conceive a high idea of it, and to approach it with a hunger like to that our Lord felt when, at the Last Supper in which He instituted it, He said to His Apostles: With desire I have desired to eat this Pasch with you before I suffer.[24] My Saviour, tell me Thyself how great is this desire of Thine, and how long it has possessed Thee; tell me why Thou hast put off satisfying it till this late hour. This desire, Thou dost reply, I have always had, for it was born with Me; for from the moment of My incarnation, having known that I was able to give Myself to My elect and unite Myself to them as food, I have desired to do so with the same ardent desire as I longed to suffer and die for them. And though My desire was always like a secret and consuming fire which nothing could extinguish, I had the patience to wait till My last hour to satisfy it, that thereby you might learn that thirty-three years of continual desires, fervent desires are well employed in preparing oneself to receive even but once the Sacrament of My body, and that those who receive it more often ought to prepare each time with as great care as if on leaving the holy table they were to pass straight from this life into eternity.

Thus does the Saviour speak to every just soul, these are the lessons He gives them; but if they desire to be inflamed with a still greater longing to receive Him, they must place before their minds every kind of mortification and virtue which Christ our Lord practises in this Sacrament, begging Him to grant them a share in these mortifications and virtues. For it is of Him that

[24] Lk 22:15

the prophet speaks when he says: *He bowed the heavens and came down: and darkness was under His feet:*[25] to bow the heavens, what is it but to communicate to men those graces and heavenly gifts which are in some sort abased and out of their place when they are found in hearts as vile and earthly as ours? But their abasement is our elevation, since they raise us from earth to Heaven and make us like to the angels. With such magnificent adornments our souls even appear like Heavens, into which the king of glory, Christ our Lord, covered with the sacramental species as with a cloud, comes as it were merely in passing; for those whom He thus visits are travellers who walk in the obscurity of faith, expecting that happy day when they shall see God clearly and face to face in His glory. But as it does not suffice, in order to communicate worthily, to know Who it is we receive, we must form the determination to labour with all our might to cut out from our heart by mortification whatever we see in it that is vicious and imperfect; above all must we put the knife to our throat, that is to say, we must repress the intemperance of the tongue and the lips, and so sanctify the day on which we have the happiness of eating this bread of angels; for the mouth and tongue which are prepared to receive the body of the Saviour ought to cast away everything which can sully or profane them.

Perhaps this is why the Holy Spirit adds these words: *Be not desirous of his meats, in which is the bread of deceit;*[26] because no man, however devoid of reason he may be, can think to eat at the same time the bread of deceit at the table of the prince of darkness and the bread of sanctity and truth at the table of the Prince of heaven. It is then absolutely necessary to abstain from the poisoned bread presented to us by the father of lies if we desire to participate in the *unleavened bread of sincerity and truth,*[27]

[25] Ps 17:10
[26] Prov 23:3
[27] 1 Cor 5:8

as says the Apostle, that is to say, with a heart sincere in its affections and true in its sentiments. And because this truth and sincerity consists principally in a very pure and lofty intention, each ought to strive after that which seems to him most perfect. St Bonaventure[28] distinguishes eight kinds of motives by which the faithful may be drawn to partake of Holy Communion.

Some, says the holy doctor, communicate because, being conscious of their spiritual infirmities, they desire the visit of the physician who alone is able to cure them; others because, having sinned deeply, they have nothing to offer to the divine justice more agreeable than this holy Victim, this Lamb without spot who taketh away the sins of the world; others because seeing themselves overwhelmed by sorrows or in the grip of violent temptations, their only hope is to have recourse to a strong and powerful God who is always ready to assist and defend them; yet others, because having some favour to ask of the eternal Father, they hope to obtain it through the merits of His Son, our only mediator. There are some who in this holy act only think to offer to the Lord the chalice of salvation out of gratitude for the benefits they have received at His hands: some only desire to honour God and His saints, by offering this oblation to Him in honour of the saints; others, urged by charity for their brethren, whether living or dead, employ the blood of Jesus to obtain for the living pardon of their sins and for the dead relief from their pains. And lastly, there are others who, consumed by the love of God, desire nothing else but that He should visit them often, that they may embrace Him with all the affection of their heart and cling closely to Him, since in Him they find all they desire, as says St Ambrose:[29] *Jesus is all in all to us.* He is indeed all in all to us: for if you desire to be healed of your wounds, He is your only physician: if you are consumed by burning fever, He is a

[28] *Process. Relig.,* c. 22
[29] Lib. 3, *de virgin, post med.*

cooling fountain; if you are weighed down by sin, He is justice; if you need help, He is your strength; do you fear death, He is life; do you desire Heaven, He is the way that leads to it; if you hate darkness, He is the light; if you are hungry, He is your nourishment. *Taste,* then, *and see that the Lord is sweet:*[30] happy is the man who hopes in Him and is but one spirit with Him.

My Jesus, my only happiness! in whom I find my All, when I possess Thee, when I am united with Thee, what more can I desire? Now I can say with the Spouse: *A cluster of cypress my love is to me, in the vineyards of Engaddi.*[31] What has the remote island of Cyprus in common with Engaddi, which is in the tribe of Juda, near the Dead Sea? From whatever angle we gaze upon our divine Spouse in this Sacrament, we can find nothing more delightful; within it is a cluster from heaven, which has an infinite number of grapes, and these grapes are the infinite number of graces with which it is filled; without, it is a delicious fruit found on our earth, whose property is to preserve health, joy and life to all those who confess the name of Christ and are dead to sin. The name *Engaddi* shows that Christ our Lord is a *fountain* in which we are washed from our sins, in which we extinguish the fire of impure passions, at which we quench our thirst; and an *eye* which conducts us safely through the dangers and temptations of this life. Would to God it were granted me to find this fountain, to cleanse myself therein and to come forth without spot or stain! Would to God I were worthy to eat of this cluster of grapes and to taste of that sweetness found in it by all holy souls in this world, so that, running swiftly on the way to Heaven, I might hope to participate one day in those eternal delights enjoyed by the company of the Blessed who reign with Jesus Christ. Amen.

[30] Ps 33:9
[31] Cant 1:13 *Botrus cypri meus mihi in vineis Engaddi. Vide* S. Hieron., *De locis Hebraicis*

Chapter IX

Of the knowledge of Christ our Lord in the glory He has in heaven, and of what He is there doing for us.

IN ORDER TO have a full and entire knowledge of Christ our Lord, it only remains to contemplate the blessed state in which He was after the resurrection, and in which He still dwells today in highest Heaven, at the right hand of His Father, infinitely exalted above the angels and endowed with every blessing for which one could wish. Let us then raise our eyes and consider Him seated on His throne in order that, as says St Paul, *we all, beholding the glory of the Lord with open face, are transformed into the same image from glory to glory.*[1] What is this glory of which the Apostle speaks, if not that of which the Saviour Himself spoke to His disciples when He told them that *Christ ought to have suffered these things, and so to enter into His glory?*[2] By His sufferings He did not obtain the glory of His soul, since He had received this at the moment of His conception; He obtained that of the body which was given to Him at His resurrection and which has always been His since His ascension into Heaven. Now this glory consists in four qualities with which His glorious body is clothed: *brightness*, which makes it appear a thousand times more luminous than the sun; *immortality*, joined with *impassibility*, so that it can no longer be touched by suffering or death; *agility*, which gives

[1] 2 Cor 3:18
[2] Lk 24:26

it wings, so to speak, with which it can fly everywhere with incredible speed and without weariness; and lastly, *subtility,* by which this body becomes *spiritual,*[3] so that, disengaged from all that is of this earth, it resembles, in some sort, a pure spirit.

Formerly he showed Himself on Mount Tabor with these same marks of glory when suddenly *His face did shine as the sun: and His garments became white as snow.*[4] St Peter was so ravished thereat, although he only caught a glimpse of one little ray of the glory with which our Lord shines in Heaven, that he could not believe there could be anything left worth seeing or desiring in this world. What would he have thought, what would he have said if in one moment all the plenitude of that light had been shown him, or if he had been allowed to enter into the abyss of the joy of his Lord and to drink from the abundant river of His sweetness?[5]

Most sweet Saviour, open Heaven to me, that I may enter in spirit and approach Thy throne, that I may contemplate the glory of Thy blessed body, and that I may be transformed into its likeness.

I

In order to begin this meditation well, we might recall to mind these words of St Paul to the Colossians: *If you be risen with Christ, seek the things that are above; where Christ is sitting at the right hand of God;*[6] the Apostle would say that no one is capable of contemplating the Son of God in the splendour of His glory and of becoming His image if he is not in truth risen with Him.

---

[3] 1 Cor 15:44
[4] Mt 17:2
[5] St Aug., *in Soliloq.,* c. 2
[6] Col 3:1

In order therefore to make ourselves like to the risen Jesus, let us first endeavour to be like the crucified Jesus. This is what the Spouse teaches us in the Canticle[7] when, having said that *a bundle of myrrh is my Beloved to me,* she immediately adds that He is as sweet as a *cluster of cypress,* showing, says St Bernard,[8] that He who in His passion is to the holy soul a bundle of myrrh, because He inspires her with thoughts and affections full of bitterness, this very same is in His resurrection like an excellent cluster of grapes, because He then excites in her thoughts and affections both sweet and consoling. It is this mysterious cluster which demonstrates to us the fertility of the true Land of Promise:[9] let us not eat of it hastily, for fear lest too great avidity should hinder us from savouring it at leisure. Our thoughts should linger on each of the glorious qualities of Jesus risen, and we should remind ourselves that this body which now shines with such brilliancy, such beauty, is the same that was once so disfigured that the prophet, seeing it in spirit, said: *There is no beauty in Him nor comeliness; and we have seen Him,… despised, and the most abject of men, a man of sorrows and acquainted with infirmity.*[10]

Face of infinite beauty, *on which the angels desire to look,*[11] because although they always see it, yet they are never weary of gazing upon it, I rejoice that Thy beauty has so many charms, that by them the celestial spirits are ravished. My soul, were it given thee to behold this divine countenance, doubtless thou wouldst remark in it wonderful traits which surpass every human imagination.

Chaste spouse of the eternal King, thou who hast the happiness of seeing Him face to face, draw for us His portrait, that

---

[7] Cant 1:12, 13
[8] Serm. 44 on the Canticle
[9] Num 113:24
[10] Is 53:2
[11] 1 Pt 1:12

we too may conceive an ardent desire of seeing Him: what sayest thou of His head, His hair, His eyes, His cheeks, His lips, His hands? *My Beloved,* she tells me, *is white and ruddy, chosen out of thousands;*[12] He possesses in an eminent degree all that is most perfect in every creature: all the beauty of earth, the sky and the stars is as nothing in comparison with His, nor is there anything in the whole world to which He can be likened. If I should say that *His head is as the finest gold: His locks as branches of palm trees, His eyes as doves upon brooks of water, washed with milk, His cheeks as aromatical spices set by the perfumers, His hands full of sapphires:* I should still say nothing which could give any idea of their excellence. O King of glory, I rejoice that Thy beauty and brilliance are such that there is nothing to which they can be compared; Most beautiful of the sons of men, have pity upon me, who am the most imperfect and loathsome of creatures: *With Thy comeliness and beauty set out, proceed prosperously, and reign*[13] for all beauty is Thine, and whatever I have proceeds from Thee. By that beauty which is in Thee, I humbly implore Thee to give me some share in it; enlighten my eyes with a ray of Thy glory, that I may know and love it; begin and fulfil in me Thy work of redemption, let love govern me in all things until I attain to Thy glorious kingdom, and *see* Thee, *the King, in Thy beauty.*[14] Amen.

After this, let us consider the other qualities of the glorified body of Jesus, reflecting in the first place on those words of St Paul, that *what things a man shall sow, those also shall he reap,*[15] and that what we reap corresponds with what we have sown. Since therefore what Christ our Lord sowed upon earth was nothing but ignominy and shame, His reaping in Heaven can only be a glory proportionate to His abasement.

[12] Cant 5:10-14
[13] Is 33:17
[14] Ps 44:5
[15] Gal 6: 8

My Saviour, what tongue is able to describe what Thou hast sowed in Thy passion and reaped in Thy resurrection? Become the prey of death, Thy body was buried in the earth like a fruitful seed; it rose immortal, not only never to die again, but to live a life of glory; it was consigned to the earth covered with wounds, it rose impassible and invulnerable; it was consigned to the earth all disfigured, weighed down and overwhelmed with woes, it rose full of beauty, agile, incapable of any suffering; it was consigned to the earth having all the weaknesses of our humanity, it rose with the vigour and subtlety of a spirit. O grain of wheat which wast sown and died in the earth, that it might *bring forth much fruit*[16] and bring forth many other grains like to itself, make me one of these precious grains which only dies in the earth in order to multiply itself the more.

The fruit of this consideration ought to be a spiritual transformation into Jesus Christ glorified, participating in His beauty by the communication of His grace, becoming resplendent as He is by faith, immortal by constant perseverance in charity, impassible by mortification, which is the sovereign remedy for every spiritual malady; agile by promptitude in fulfilling God's commands, and carrying out His inspirations and counsels; lastly becoming wholly spiritual by so absolute a command over the flesh and its passions, that having no longer anything in common with the things of sense, *our conversation may be in Heaven.*[17] For this is the means by which we may obtain for our own bodies the glorious qualities of the body of our Redeemer, and of being able to say with the Apostle: *Our conversation is in Heaven; from whence also we look for the Saviour, our Lord Jesus Christ, Who will reform the body of our lowness, made like to the body of His glory.*[18] For if we are already in this life trans-

[16] Cf. Jn 12:24
[17] Phil 3:20
[18] *Ibid*

formed spiritually into Him, we shall be so corporally also in the next;[19] He will bring about in our souls a transformation like to that which ought to take place in our bodies on the day of resurrection; and although according to the flesh we shall be buried in the earth, we shall live according to the spirit a holy and happy life with Jesus Christ in heaven.

II

Although Christ our Lord is seated in highest Heaven on the throne of His glory, and there rests from all His former labours and tastes their fruit in His own natural body, yet for all that we must not imagine that He watches with less solicitude over the welfare of His mystical body, which is the Church, composed of all the faithful and particularly of the elect. Even in this place of repose He is not idle, He acts continually, but in a tranquil manner, without emotion, uneasiness or trouble.

In the first place, He exercises the office of *advocate* of men, and in order to justify them fully before His heavenly Father, He applies to them the merits of His passion and death. *If any man sin,* says the beloved disciple, *we have an advocate with the Father, Jesus Christ the just, and He is the propitiation for our sins: and not for ours only, but also for those of the whole world.*[20] And what will be His qualities as Advocate? He is most wise in His knowledge of our necessities, most prudent in applying admirable counsels and remedies, very vigilant in procuring them for us, most merciful in His compassion for our trials and most powerful in obtaining for us the cure of all our spiritual diseases. For being holy, or rather holiness itself, He has no need to plead for Himself; and as besides He has already satisfied for

[19] St Greg., *in Cant.,* 1
[20] 1 Jn 2:1

our sins by the shedding of His blood, He has only to show His wounds to the Father of mercies to obtain His favour for us. The great Apostle also tells us that Jesus is entered *into Heaven itself, that He may appear now in the presence of God for us.*[21] So that if the divine justice, irritated against a sinner, should say to His ministers: *Behold, for these three years I am come seeking fruit on this fig tree, and I find none. Cut it down therefore: why cumbereth it the ground?*[22] our charitable Advocate will answer: *Let it alone this year also, until I dig about it, and dung it. And if happily it bear fruit.*[23] His intercession has such power that divine justice will suspend the execution of the sentence against the sinner until it has been proved whether there is still chance of amendment; the excess of His charity induces Him to offer Himself to labour at the root of the barren fig tree and do everything that is possible to enable it to bear fruit.

My most sweet and loving Advocate! I confess myself to be a barren fig tree, deserving to be accursed and dug up by the rigour of Thy divine justice; but let Thy mercy intercede for me; fertilise me by whatever remedies Thou dost judge fitting, however painful and violent they may be, that cultivated by Thy hands, I may bring forth such fruit as my heavenly Father requires from me. Amen.

To this office, which belongs to Christ our Lord as man, He has added another from which we gain great profit, and that is to be the supreme *Almoner* of God: for indeed all the alms which are asked from the eternal Father are asked in the name of His Son, through whom the Father dispenses them. He even puts into His hands whatever petitions we present to Him, for He has put all things into His hands, and all the blessings and spiritual alms which descend from heaven descend from

[21] Heb 9:24
[22] Lk 15:7
[23] *Ibid*, 8

the hands of Jesus Christ and are by Him distributed to the poor and needy. Therefore it may be said that Christ our Lord seated on His throne is continually occupied in receiving our petitions, listening to our sighs, and imparting to us His gifts with the greatest liberality and mercy, as we have said above.

But His liberality is not limited merely to those things which we ask from Him, it extends also to all the spiritual gifts which proceed from the Father of lights and to all those special graces which He communicates to His elect. *Blessed be the God and Father of our Lord Jesus Christ,* cries St Paul, *who hath blessed us with spiritual blessings in heavenly places in Christ.*[24] For all these things come to us by the hands of Jesus Christ, who, as the same Apostle says further on, ascending on high, *gave gifts to men,*[25] distributing them with such equity and justice that each receives all those graces and helps of which he has need, according to his capacity. And, what is above all, He pours down upon them the greatest of all His gifts, the Holy Ghost Himself, as He did upon His Apostles; He sends this sanctifying Spirit as often as they are disposed to receive Him, Himself aiding them to obtain these good dispositions. He also inspires them with many holy thoughts, by which He produces in them an infinite number of admirable results; for it is He who by His Spirit governs the whole Church; He is the head and master of all the faithful; He is the only shepherd of this great flock; nothing can be accomplished apart from Him, and it is only by His help that each is able to acquit himself of his ministry.

From this we may see that the third office which our Lord fulfils for us in heaven is that of supreme *Governor* of the universal Church: He acts as sovereign Pontiff with the popes, His Vicars; He decides, He ordains, He performs with them all the

[24] Eph 1:3
[25] Eph 4:8

duties of their charge. He fulfils the office of bishop and pastor with the bishops and other pastors of souls. He fulfils the office of priest with the priests and confessors; He offers the sacrifice of the Mass along with them and descends from heaven as Victim; they are His mouthpieces at the altar and in the tribunal of penance, and it is in His name that they say: *This is my body. I absolve you from your sins.* He performs the office of preaching with preachers, He instructs them interiorly, He suggests to them what to say and puts the words into their mouths; for it is not they who speak, but the Spirit of God who speaks in them. He fulfils the office of director with directors of souls, He inspires them with what they ought to teach, and Himself secretly instils the corresponding grace of understanding into the souls under their guidance. He prays with those who pray, meditate or contemplate and He Himself forms them in the exercise of prayer. And if they find themselves in danger, or in the midst of enemies, He shows Himself to them as He did to St Stephen, ever ready to succour and defend them.

What more can we say of this loving Saviour? Is He not also the supreme *Steward* of His heavenly Father? Since it is His office also to pay and remunerate the just both in this life and the next for the service they have rendered, we may call Him the supreme *Procurator,* to whom the lord of the vineyard saith: *Call the labourers, and give them their hire.*[26] He pays them liberally with spiritual consolations and by the fresh progress in virtue which He enables them to make: oftentimes He even rewards them with gratuitous graces and extraordinary favours; He returns a hundredfold to all those who have left all for His love;[27] He communicates to whom He will the gift of perseverance; finally, He awards crowns to those whom He judges worthy. This was revealed to the author of the fourth

[26] Mt 20:8
[27] Cf. Mt 19:29

book of Esdras from which the Church herself accepts some verses: *I saw,* he says, *on Mount Sion a great multitude, which no one could number, and all praised the Lord with canticles. And in the midst of them was a young man, of great stature, taller than all the rest, and he was placing crowns on all their heads, and was greatly exalted; but I was astonished at the sight. Then I questioned the Angel and said: Who are these, Lord? Who answered and said to me: These are they who have put off the tunic of mortality and put on that of immortality, and have confessed the name of God: now they are crowned and receive palms. And I said to the angel: This young man, who is he, that places crowns on their heads and palms in their hands? And he answering said to me: This is the Son of God, whom they have confessed in the world.*[28] Therefore doth He reward them for their labours.

O only-begotten Son of the living God, I rejoice that Thou hast around Thee so many men worthy to participate in Thy glory; grant me grace to serve Thee so faithfully that I may deserve to be crowned by Thy hand and to enjoy Thee for ever in Thy kingdom. Amen.

We seem to have forgotten the office of *Judge,* which nevertheless this same Lord exercises over men, not only rewarding the good, but even in this life chastising the wicked, passing sentence upon them at the moment of death, and condemning them to punishment according to the measure of their guilt. This office He will continue to exercise until the day of universal judgement, when He will return visibly to earth with great majesty to judge all men after their resurrection: casting sinners from Him into eternal fire, but calling the just to go with Him into eternal joy.

But because we have spoken at length of this judgement

---

[28] 4 Esdras 2:42 (This book is not accepted by the Council of Trent as canonical. Translator's note.) Cf. Apoc 7:9

in another place,[29] it will be enough to add here that since the Judge Himself will open and manifest to all the book of His holy life, and those things which are written therein[30] for the condemnation of sinners who would neither read nor practise what is taught in it, reason demands, says St Gregory,[31] that we should apply ourselves to it now, and make it our principal study.

It is also of great importance to read diligently those authors who treat of the mystical life and to practise those virtues which they specially recommend, in order to attain to that perfection which we may easily learn in that first of all books which is the divine essence.

[29] Part I, Med. 13, etc
[30] Apoc 5:9
[31] *Lib.* 24 *Mor.,* c. 6

Chapter X

Of that union with God by knowledge and love which is proper to the unitive way; and of its stupendous properties and effects.

IN THE PRECEDING treatises we have sufficiently explained all that regards the way called *unitive,* which, according to St Paul, is to become one spirit with God: *He who is joined to the Lord is one spirit.*[1] Since we have already said so many and various things about it, as occasion required, we will now make a kind of recapitulation, or epilogue, of the most essential qualities of this divine union, by which the soul usually rises to the heights of perfect contemplation. Taking for granted, then, what has already been said in the twelfth chapter of the second treatise of this work,[2] let us first of all remark that the three divine Persons are united with just souls in two different manners.

The first of these is *habitual* and permanent, and is the result of sanctifying grace, of the habit of charity, of the infused virtues and the gifts of the Holy Ghost which are inseparable from them: on God's part, it never fails, and it is always in our power to preserve it by avoiding mortal sin. For *the gifts of God,* as says the Apostle, *are without repentance,*[3] and as long as we desire His love He will never take them from us. Moreover, the Lord Himself has said: *If anyone love Me, he will keep My word, and My Father will love him, and We will come to him,*

---

[1] 1 Cor 6:17
[2] Chapter II of the present volume.
[3] Rom 11:29

and will make our abode with him,[4] *and I will ask the Father and He will give you another Paraclete, that He may abide with you for ever;*[5] and, as St John says: *God is charity: and he that abideth in charity, abideth in God, and God in him,*[6] for as long as created charity abides in the soul, uncreated charity, which is God Himself, remains also: and although the soul may be very imperfect and forgetful of the grace it has received, yet God is still with it, keeping it united with Himself.

The other kind of union, which is the most perfect, is what is called *actual* union, in virtue of which the most holy Trinity abides in these just souls, impelling them to produce acts of charity and of the other virtues they have received, so that they know Him actually, and love Him as perfectly as the precept of charity requires: *Thou shalt love the Lord thy God with thy whole heart, and with thy whole soul, and with thy whole strength,*[7] *and with thy whole mind.*[8] But it must be remarked that this union is not continuous, but is only enjoyed at intervals and at certain seasons when it pleases the Lord to visit His friends. For although this grace may at times be granted to all the just, yet the unitive way belongs properly only to perfect souls, who alone can be said to be in the state of union. They alone bring the necessary dispositions to enjoy this divine union frequently, for they alone know how to co-operate with the divine work in all that depends upon themselves.

This co-operation consists principally in recollecting and bringing into play, with the help of God, all those faculties which concur in the union of love: that is, the heart, the soul, and the mind, with all the other powers of body and spirit. For

[4] Jn 14:23
[5] *Ibid*, 16
[6] 1 Jn 4:16
[7] Deut 6:5, Mt 22:37
[8] Lk 10:27

if they obtain union and concord among themselves, there will presently follow union with God Himself, who has said: *Where there are two or three gathered together in my name, there am I in the midst of them.*[9] What are these three, asks St Jerome, but the body, soul and spirit?[10] But when do they act in this manner? It is when the body, recollecting all its senses, motions and powers, is peacefully obedient to the soul, and the soul itself, which is the sensitive part, recollects and unites all its imaginations, and its sensitive appetite, keeping them so well bridled that they act only and according to the impulse of the spirit; this spirit, again, which is the reasonable part, unites the memory, understanding and will so closely to God, that they cannot dissipate themselves on any other object; when the whole man has thus resolved to omit nothing on his part to maintain this union between all his powers, God Himself descends into the midst of them, that He may bind them yet more closely among themselves and unite them to Himself by the union of actual love, which is the most perfect kind of love, and which forms the matter of the first precept of His law. For the *memory* is united with God, being actually mindful of His divine presence; the *understanding* is united with God, knowing His infinite greatness and majesty; the *will* is united with the same Lord, loving and embracing His immense bounty, on which its gaze is steadily fixed. It is the same with the imagination, which portrays to itself in a lively and agreeable manner the infinite perfections of its God, the appetite ardently desires the beauties it thus perceives; the senses and the very body itself participate by a sweet communication in the joys of the soul, and endeavour to the utmost of their power not to trouble or disturb it.

In this way, as long as it lasts, the whole man is occupied in loving God, with heart, and mind, and soul, and strength,

---

[9] Mt 18:20; *idem dicit* St Ambrose., lib. 7, in Luc. 13
[10] St Jerome, *in hoc loc.*

with all his energies, so that he then experiences that happy state which God promised by the mouth of Jeremias, saying: *He shall sit solitary and hold his peace; because he hath taken it upon himself;*[11] for this union is wont to effect a stupendous quietude, solitude, silence and suspension or elevation above all things created. O happy quiet, which compels the spirit to rise up to God: happy solitude, which keeps company with the most holy Trinity; happy silence, in which God speaks, and man holds his peace: though if man does then speak, it is with God alone. O happy suspension, which suspends the labours of the body, that the spirit alone may work; O happy elevation, which unites the spirit of man to that of God, and causes man, created in the image of the three divine Persons, to participate, after a certain fashion, in the ineffable union which They have among themselves!

Most holy and adorable Trinity, vouchsafe to admit me into that most glorious union which Thou hast in Thyself: that the three powers of my soul may be united with Thee, as the Three Persons are in Thy divine essence. O Son of the living God, who didst ask that Thy faithful *might be one, as Thou and the Father are one*:[12] teach me how this union may be brought about, and what I must do to render myself less unworthy of it.

I. *Of six properties belonging to the union wrought by charity*

That we may understand more clearly the nature of this union, and how it is wrought principally in the three superior powers of the soul, on which is impressed the image of the most holy Trinity, it will be well to explain here in some detail what concerns each one of these powers.

[11] *Sedebit solitarius et tacebit: quia levavit super se.* Lam 3:28
[12] Cf. Jn 17:22

Let us begin with the will, in which resides charity and on which divine love has special power to work. St Denis[13] says that one of the properties of this love is to cause ecstasies and transports, by means of which the soul, as it were, goes out of itself; that it now only lives in the object of its love, and that thus the will, ceasing to be its own, is entirely attached to God, according to these words: *Where thy treasure is, there is thy heart also.*[14] But since there are two kinds of love, the one called *concupiscence*, which regards nothing in the object of its love save its own interest; the other, which is called *friendship* or *benevolence*, by which we love our friend for that good which he has in himself; we must exclude from fervent contemplation the first of these loves, which cannot but be very imperfect, since it has its root in self-love, and if it goes outside itself to seek those advantages which are lacking to it, it speedily returns, to consider everything in the light of its own welfare, and only so far as they are useful to itself.

It is then only disinterested love which can accord with the highest contemplation, in which the will goes altogether out of itself,[15] in order to be intimately united with God for Himself alone and for His infinite goodness and beauty, in which it finds repose and perfect contentment. It is indeed so fully satisfied that it is no longer mindful of itself nor of its bodily requirements, nor of its senses nor commodities, still less does it think of any reward. All these things for the time being are so remote from it that it becomes like a stranger to itself, content with God alone. For this love is so ardent that by a sweet violence it draws after it the understanding and the memory, so that both these also are only occupied with the thought and

---

[13] C. 4, *De divin. nomin.*, p. 1; St Thom., *S. Th.* IIa-IIae, Q. 28, art. 3, et IIa-IIae, Q. 185, art. 2

[14] Mt 6:21

[15] *Sive mente excedimus Deo.* 2 Cor 5:13

remembrance of the Beloved. The Holy Spirit, who is uncreated charity, works all these effects in it by a wondrous strength and sweetness, according to that saying of St Paul: *the charity of God is poured forth in our hearts, by the Holy Ghost, who is given to us.*[16] In saying that it is 'poured forth' St Paul shows the manner in which He fills and penetrates the depths of the soul, that is to say, the spiritual powers, to which He is intimately united. This is that most excellent charity so much esteemed by the Holy Fathers and spiritual men who have experienced it, and whose properties, as says Richard of St Victor,[17] are so admirable.

First, the soul which has acquired this divine charity cleaves only to God; it embraces Him so closely by love and knowledge, which are its two arms, that for no created thing will it leave Him, nor will it ever depart from His presence, saying with the Spouse: *I have found him whom my soul loveth: I held Him, and I will not let Him go:*[18] and again: *A bundle of* very fragrant *myrrh is my beloved to me, He shall abide between my breasts;*[19] for I will place Him between my memory and my will, being continually mindful of Him, that I may constantly love Him above all things; and by His sweet presence He shall communicate to me the incorruptibility of myrrh. *Hence* it comes that this *charity will be insatiable;* never will it be satisfied with knowing and thinking of its Beloved, nor of offering Him all the service it can; all its desire is to do and to suffer whatever is most painful, that it may grow in the love of a God so sovereignly lovable; lastly, it burns with an interior fire which never says: *It is enough,* because its love is never as ardent as it desires.[20] Therefore, with a holy jealousy, it longs to love Him

[16] Rom 5:5
[17] *De grad. charitatis*
[18] Cant 3:4
[19] *Ibid.* 1:12
[20] Prov 30:16

and to serve Him as much as all the saints together have loved Him and served Him; for, when it is question of the fervour of love, it would excel, if possible, all others put together. O most heroic virtue! You have learnt the art of stealing innocently from others whatever they have of good, and to make it your own without robbing them; yet even after that, you are not fully content!

Hence it is that this *charity* is also *invincible*. For, being united with God, it can do all things and it overcomes all things without being afraid of anything. For, as we have said above,[21] *Love is strong as death, nor can the floods drown* its flames.[22] And indeed, it would rather die than cease to love. For although death takes away the life of the body, and with it cease faith and hope, which are imperfect virtues: *yet charity never faileth*.[23] For by charity we love God, whether in this life by faith only we see Him; or whether we behold Him face to face by the light of glory; whether we possess Him as yet only by faith, or are fully united with Him in eternity. *Whosoever* therefore thus embraces Him, is *vehemently* delighted with the most pure and chaste delights; for He who loves vehemently cannot behold the object of His love without experiencing a most sensible joy. He cries out with holy David: *I remembered God, and was delighted;*[24] or with the Spouse: *The king hath brought me into his store-rooms: we will be glad and rejoice in thee, remembering thy breasts more than wine.*[25] Although he is alone, he says in the plural *we will be glad,* to show that all his powers and all his senses participate in this joy, that they taste the most pure milk which flows from the bosom of God, and which exceeds

[21] Ch. 6
[22] Cant 8:6
[23] 1 Cor 13:8
[24] Ps 76:4
[25] Cant 1:3

beyond all comparison the wine of earthly consolations. If he should sometimes dwell on the pleasures of the world, it is not in order to seek them, but, on the contrary, to conceive a great contempt for them, since he no longer esteems nor desires any save those which come from heaven. Yet neither does he set his happiness in these, for nothing created can now satisfy him: he cries out that he rejoices in nought *but Thee,* my God, my beloved and all my joy. For Thou art my only delight, my only joy: all my happiness consists in seeing myself united with Thee, my only consolation lies in pleasing Thee: *For what have I in heaven? And besides Thee what do I desire upon earth?*[26] Thou art all my inheritance, in Thee all my happiness and felicity consist.

Nevertheless, it must not be imagined that the sweetnesses of divine love are never mingled with any bitterness. Let us listen to the holy Spouse who addresses to her companions these tender words: *I adjure you, daughters of Jerusalem, if you find my beloved, that you tell him that I languish with love,*[27] or as the Septuagint translates: *I am wounded by charity.* For the wound of love is not without its torment, though charity renders it so sweet that he desires never to be without this wound as long as he lives. For the wounds of charity are violent desires of *loving* and *pleasing God,* so that the impossibility of doing all he would wish causes him to suffer a kind of sweet martyrdom; he longs to see all nations adore and glorify God; and his desires become so fervent that he cannot contain himself at the sight of the continual insults offered to his Beloved; he suffers also a *holy impatience* to go to God, and to enjoy Him in glory without any fear of ever losing Him again or falling from grace; these desires often cause him to break out into loving complaints, because the happiness he so ardently desires is so long delayed.

[26] Ps 72:25
[27] Cant 5:8

Hence it is that as one who has received a mortal wound, or who suffers from burning thirst, thinks of nothing but how he can obtain relief; so a soul whose heart is transpierced by the dart of love, or which burns with love for God, cannot be one moment without thinking of Him, and while it thus thinks, it *makes*, according to the saying of David, *its tears into bread;*[28] it sends forth continual sighs and prayers to heaven to assure its loving Spouse that it languishes with love. All the creatures it sees around it seem to speak of the Beloved, Who is present though unseen, and Who from all sides shoots into its heart burning arrows of love; in this way it keeps the Beloved always before its eyes, and the sight of all His good gifts causes continual yearnings to be for ever united with Him. The lover's own good works serve in no small degree to keep his Beloved in mind, since he knows well that without Him he can do nothing. *Come,* he says, *my Beloved, let us go forth into the field;*[29] let us labour together, Thou with me and I with Thee; I will look upon Thee as Thou dost look on me: do Thou assist me, so that I may ever work and labour as Thou wouldst have me do.

II. Of six other wonders which accompany this union of love

We have now seen the excellent qualities of the love which is called *unitive;* it is impossible to consider them attentively without confessing how *admirable* it is, because whatever such a lover thinks, or desires, all he says, all he does, all he suffers for God shows an extraordinary fervour; so also a soul thus enamoured by this divine fire becomes more and more inflamed until, like a burning flame, it rises to Heaven with such

[28] Ps 41:4
[29] Cant 7:11

impetuosity that the blessed spirits cry out in astonishment: *Who is this that cometh up from the desert, flowing with delights, leaning upon her beloved?*[30]

O holy angels, tell us what it is in this which so astonishes you, that we may see if there is anything we can imitate. Many things, they reply, surprise us: *first,* we admire that a soul still clothed with its earthly body and dragged down by its carnal inclinations, should yet overcome its natural propensities and utterly forsake itself, in order to ascend and have its conversation in Heaven, dwelling in spirit where it cannot yet come in the body. In the *second* place, we wonder that being still on the earth, where sensual pleasures alone are wont to be sought, this soul lives as in a desert, always alone, an enemy to the world, always recollected in itself, conversing with God alone in this sweet solitude.

Thirdly, we admire that although it has risen so high, and although the flesh separates itself with such pain from all that gives it satisfaction, yet this soul renounces its flesh and itself utterly, so as to advance without stopping on the path to heaven, without ever turning back or resting, or growing weary until it reaches the apex of its desires.

But *lastly,* what surprises us most of all is that this wonderful love permits it to act so familiarly with the Beloved that it dares to lean upon Him, and He sustains her with His all-powerful hand.

Celestial spirits, we recognise now that you have great reason to be astonished that so feeble a creature should have the courage to do such great things for its Creator; but allow us to ask you again if you are not surprised at seeing it mount up to Heaven, full of holy delights? You answer us that this is less marvellous because, having renounced the pleasures of sense,

[30] Cant 8:5

it is but natural that the Beloved should enable it to taste those of the spirit. Would it be possible for it to rise, as it has done, above all that flatters the body, if it had not already entered into the joys of its Lord? Would it experience such eagerness to be united with Him, if it had not begun to drink of the torrent of delights? It sees Him whom it loves, it feels Him, it embraces Him, and it leans upon Him. Is it surprising that when He rises, it follows Him, since it is so intimately united with Him and He dwells in it, and that, knit together by a reciprocal love, they are no longer two, but one same spirit?

Most holy Spirit, draw me far away from all created things, that I may ascend by contemplation to unite myself with Thee, my Creator, leaning ever upon Thee, not upon myself; give me so clear a knowledge of what Thou art that I may grow in love, *ascending from strength to strength, until the God of gods shall be seen in Sion.*[31] Amen.

There is yet another effect of divine grace to be admired in this soul which *rises from the desert filled with delights*; it is that it does not lean upon these extraordinary favours, nor upon its own virtue, but upon the help of the Beloved. For it is almost a miracle to be filled with heavenly consolations and yet not put one's confidence in them nor have any attachment to them. But when a soul attains to the perfect contemplation of God, the more it enjoys Him, and by enjoying Him, knows Him the more, it also comes to know itself better, and to be convinced that the singular favours it enjoys are in no way due to its own merits. Therefore is it very careful to take no credit for them to itself, nor to find its support either in them or in itself: yet it does not belittle them, not on account of the sensible joy they produce, but because it draws from them ever greater motives for loving God, and ever more certain proofs of God's

[31] Cf. Ps 83:8

goodness towards it, and of the pleasure He takes in showing by such tokens how much He loves it. On the other hand, such a soul loves its God so much that even without these visible proofs of affection it would never cease to strive to rise from the desert to go to Him and to grow in virtue, just by strength of desire to please Him and to converse familiarly with Him. Souls like this, indeed, are prone to believe that their slender merits could never deserve the transports of joy and love of which we have spoken;[32] yet they will never cease to strive to overcome their weakness and to do all in their power for the glory of the Beloved; they desire indeed to do even infinitely more, and leave no stone unturned to reach the highest possible point of perfection.

III. Of the manner in which knowledge and love effect the most intimate union between God and the soul

There still remains something to be considered in this union, so wholly divine; it lies in this, that not only does it ravish the celestial spirits with admiration, but it gains the heart of God Himself: so that a soul wounded by the dart of charity causes a like wound to the Spouse, and, burning with the same flame of love, they are continually mindful of one another. God is ever thinking how to enrich the soul with His gifts: the soul meanwhile is occupied entirely with the glory of God: *My Beloved,* it says, *to me, and I to Him;*[33] I am united with Him and He with me; I think of Him and He of me: He provides for my wants while I am consumed in His service. My love for Him is an arrow which pierces my heart, His love for me is one still more sharp which pierces His own. But who would dare

[32] Richard of St Victor, B. 4, *De Contemp.,* ch. 10
[33] Cant 2:16

to speak thus unless God Himself had said to the spouse: *Thou hast wounded my heart, my sister, my spouse, thou hast wounded my heart with one of thy eyes, and with one hair of thy neck?*[34]

The *eyes* of a soul that is occupied with the life of contemplation are, as we have already said, knowledge and love; its *hairs* are the thoughts which come forth in crowds from the memory. If all these are in perfect harmony, the memory and the understanding recollect their thoughts in God in order that the will may love Him more: in Him and for Him the will unites all its affections, that the mind may know Him better; it is this union which inflicts on the heart a very deep wound. For just as arrows are loosed from the bow with violence and so penetrate the body and remain deeply embedded; so one may say that knowledge and love enter into the very bosom of God and that there, joining with one another, they are united also with Him; because neither knowledge alone nor love alone are able to effect this union, which even in Heaven, and still more on earth, is the common product of both together. It is then that God, whose heart is wounded, burns with love for the soul which gazes upon Him with these two eyes, and which never turns its look upon any object capable of arousing any impure thought.

Of all this we have an instructive figure in those two great friends of Jesus, Saints Peter and John, who set out together to seek the risen Saviour. *They both ran together, and that other disciple did outrun Peter, and came first to the sepulchre... yet he went not in. Then cometh Simon Peter, following him, and went into the sepulchre, and saw the linen cloths lying,* and the other things that were in the sepulchre; *then that other disciple also went in, who first came to the sepulchre: and he saw and believed;* and going away from the tomb, *they departed again to their home.*[35] What is signified by all this unless that knowledge and love, represented

[34] Cant 4:9
[35] Jn 20:4

by the two disciples, set out together in the search for God? At the start their pace is the same, and they keep side by side; but love, symbolised by John, having greater fervour, gains upon the other little by little, and reaches first the gates of Heaven where dwells Him whom they seek. It cries out, it sighs, it knocks, it is all impatience for union with the Beloved: at its cries, its tears, the *eternal gates*[36] are opened to knowledge, figured by Peter. Then, in a manner unknown before, it enters Heaven, even into God Himself; it sees, it contemplates, it admires the greatness and the marvellous works of this *King of Glory*. And then love enters also: it runs to the Beloved; it embraces Him and by many tender affections it tastes more than ever before that God is sweet. Thus does love augment faith and perfect knowledge, giving it new means of searching and penetrating yet more deeply; for, as says St Augustine, the more we love God, the better we know Him, and love only enters into the heart of God that it may know Him and love Him yet more.[37]

Then Peter and John, these two faithful friends, these two inseparable companions, shut themselves up in the bosom of the Divinity as in a glorious sepulchre, until it shall be time to come forth. But when they do come forth, whither should they go unless to *their own homes*,[38] thinking over and pondering what they have seen? Peter especially *went away wondering in himself*,[39] nor could he ever cease to admire the magnificent mysteries which had been revealed to him. In the same way may we conserve our union with God, going over again and again in our mind what we have learnt in the eternal source of light, and bringing forth fruits of incredible sweetness and delight.

---

[36] Ps 23:7

[37] Book 8, *De Trinit.*, cap. penult.; and Book 38 QQ., Q. xxxv. St Thom. I-II, Q. xxviii, art. 2

[38] *Ad semetipsos*

[39] Lk 24:12

APPENDIX
Some Prayers from the "Meditations"

I. A PRAYER FOR CHRISTMAS

Most exalted yet most humbled Babe
In all things to be adored
In all things loved
Quanto pro me vilior
Tanto mihi carior
The more Thou art despised for me
The more worthy art Thou to be loved.
The more Thou art humble
The more to be exalted.
Teach me to love Thee as Thou deservest
To demean and humble myself
As I deserve.
To demean myself in Thee
Is to exalt myself in Thee.
Jesus I am all confounded
Seeing Thee so great
Yet so humbled
Myself so vile
Yet so proud.
Holy Child
Teach me to humble myself.
He that humbles himself with Thee on earth
Shall by Thee be exalted in Heaven.
Amen.

II. BENEDICTUS QUI VENIT

Sweet Jesus
Soften the hardness of our hearts
Convert them to Thyself
That we may acknowledge Thee, our Saviour
Blessed is He that cometh
In the Name of the Lord
To save us
Save us all dear Saviour
Be not unmindful of my heart
Though it be harder than stone
Soften it, move it
Make it tender and supple
Fill it with the spirit of devotion
So that I may ever pray to Thee
Ever love Thee and ever laud Thee
World without end.
Amen.

III. BLESSED ARE THEY THAT MOURN

Sweet Jesus
Dost Thou weep for my miseries
Forgetful of Thine own?
My soul
Dost thou not weep
Seeing this Child weep
Who weepeth for thee?
Weep for compassion seeing Him weep
Weep because thou dost cause Him to weep
Weep for thy sins
Which afflict His heart

If this does not make thee weep
Then weep for thy own hard heart
That cannot weep
Having so much reason for tears.
Sacred Virgin
Obtain for me the gift of tears
That I may weep with thee
That I may comfort thy Son
Who is comforted to see us weep
For He said
Blessed are they that mourn
For they shall be comforted.
Amen.

IV. IGNIS ARDENS

Jesus Christ
Constant lover of souls;
The fire that burns in Thee
No water of tribulation can extinguish
Nor torments quench.
How often have I endeavoured
By my sins and ingratitude
To put out its flames?
My Saviour
Thou hast always prevailed
Ever returning good
To one who served Thee evilly
Casting hot coals upon his heart
Who daily multiplied offences.
My Saviour
Cease not to love me to the end
However ill I repay Thee

That so I may love Thee also
Through endless ages.
Amen.

V. MY HONOUR

Christ my glory
I desire no greater honour
Than to honour Thee
For Thy honour
Is my honour
That Thou be honoured by all
Is my greatest honour
If Thou be pleased to honour Thyself
With my dishonours
This also I will hold
For a very high honour
That so I may glorify Thee
Who art worthy of infinite honour
World without end.
Amen.

VI. THE PRESENCE OF GOD

Most sweet Lord
If Thou be with me
What can be wanting to me?
Invisible God
Grant me ever to live in Thy presence
Let me keep Thee before my eyes
As if I saw Thee before me
Thou art my Father

Leave me not an orphan
Thou art my Comforter
Leave me not sorrowing
With Thee I can do all things
Without Thee nothing whatever
Spur on my slothfulnes
Let me realise Thy presence
Say to my soul
I am always with thee
In thy labours to strengthen thee
In thy duties to assist thee
In all thy works to judge thee
And reward thee
I will be with thee everywhere
Unless thou separate thyself from Me.
Amen.

VII. QUID RETRIBUAM?

Jesus my dear Saviour
How infinite is Thy liberality
Opening wide both hands
To fill us with blessings and virtues.
Thyself whole and entire
Thou givest for our ransom
Making Thyself our food, our companion
Freely
With no profit to Thyself
Just because Thou art so good and liberal
Humbly I crave, Lord
To kiss and venerate Thy hands
I thank Thee for all Thy favours

I glorify Thee for all the wonders
These hands have wrought.
Amen.

VIII. DA QUOD JUBES ET JUBE QUOD VIS

My well-Beloved
Make me fulfil the will of Thy Father
In like manner as Thou didst
Loving Him as Thou hast loved Him
That I may be loved by Him
Even as Thou art
Let me love Thee
As Thou hast loved me
Since Thou commandest me to love Thee
Give what Thou commandest
That I may love Thee
As Thou desirest.
Amen.

IX. TUUS SUM EGO, SALVUM ME FAC

Heavenly Father
Have care of my body and soul
Of all my senses and faculties
Because they are Thine
Preserve and nourish
The desires and good purposes
With which Thou hast inspired me
For they also are Thine
And who is he that will not care
For that which is his own?
Tuus sum ego, salvum me fac

I am Thine, save Thou me
My soul is Thine
Save it
My understanding is Thine
Illuminate it
My will is thine
Govern it
Lord Jesus
Never let me belong to that world
For which Thou didst not pray
If I am shut out from Thy prayer
I shall be excluded also
From Thy kingdom.
Amen.

IX. A PETITION

Christ my Lord
Where two or three are gathered together
In Thy Name
Thou hast promised to be with them
Gather together in holy prayer
My three powers
Memory, understanding and will
Come then Lord
Set Thyself in the midst of them
Thou art their Sun
Let Thy light shine upon them
Thou art their Master
Instruct and teach them
Thou art their Protector
Defend and govern them
Shelter them under the shadow of Thy wings

Unite Thyself with them
In the union of perfect love.
Amen.

X. INCLINA CŒLOS ET DESCENDE

Eternal God
It is Thy gracious pleasure
To make my poor soul Thy home
See how little it is
How narrow and poor
Wanting all beauty and grace
Enlarge it with Thy gifts
I beseech Thee
Replenish it with Thy charity
Adorn it with Thine own virtues
Inclina cœlos tuos et descende
Make a starry Heaven of my heart
Let me become Thy dwelling-place.
Amen.

XII. CHRISTUS REX

Ecce rex tuus venit tibi
Would that I well and rightly understood
Who this my King is
And in what manner He comes
Thou my Saviour art my King
King of kings
King of men
King of Angels
King of Heaven and Earth
Absolute Monarch of all things

Yet hast Thou come from Heaven for me
For my salvation and consolation
For my remedy and example
For my defence and my protection
Thou art my King and my Beloved
Thou to me and I to Thee
Henceforth I dedicate myself to Thee
To Thy service, honour and glory
To obey Thee, love Thee, adore Thee
To be wholly Thine
Since Thou art wholly mine
As Thou comest to me
Poor, meek and humble
So will I go forth to meet Thee
In poverty, meekness and humility
Wearing Thine own livery.
Amen.

XI. CHRIST'S CAPTIVE

Behold my Redeemer
I humbly cast at Thy feet
All I have, all my honour
Myself wholly
All my wishes and desires
Tread and trample on me, Lord
Dispose of me just as Thou wilt
Triumph over me
Who have been Thy enemy
I will carry the palm of Thy victory
In my own hands
Gladly will I publish it
Throughout the world

For to be conquered by Thee
Is indeed Thy victory
But how great a gain for me
Since it is also my victory
Because it is Thine.
Amen.

XII. PANIS ANGELORUM

Celestial food
Bread of Angels
Daily bread
Let me so eat Thee day by day
That I may live as an angel upon earth
A life celestial and divine
Wine springing forth virgins
Cheering the heart of man
Come I beseech Thee
Purify me with Thy own purity
Nourish the life of my soul
Conserve and fortify it
Inebriate it and make it glad
With the force of Thy divine love.
Amen.

XIII. CALIX TUUS INEBRIANS

Most precious Blood of Jesus
Shed in Gethsemane
From all the pores of His body
With such deep sadness and agony of soul
I rejoice to see Thee
Gathered into this chalice

To be adored by all the faithful.
I adore and glorify Thee
As much as I am able.
Vouchsafe to deliver me
I beseech Thee
From those eternal agonies and pains
Which my sins have deserved
Since it was for them
That Thou wast shed.
Amen.

II

Most precious chalice
Full of the Blood of my Lord Jesus
Which streamed down from His shoulders
All torn with whips and scourges
Which poured too from His sacred head
Pierced with most sharp thorns
Inebriate me
I beseech Thee
With the wine of this most precious Blood
That I may be wholly changed
Into His love
Who shed it for love of me.
Amen.

III

Most loving Jesus
Thou hast placed in this chalice
That Blood Thou didst shed on the cross
From the wounds of Thy hands and feet
And from Thy pierced side

What shall I render Thee
My Lord
For so great a benefit
But only this selfsame Blood
In this chalice of my salvation
Glorifying thereby Thy holy Name.
Amen.

XIV. LIVING BREAD

My God
Immense yet invisible
Most present yet most absent
Sometimes Thou so hidest Thyself
As to seem very far away
Sometimes Thou showest Thyself
As verily present
Come Lord to my soul
Visit her with Thy sweet presence
Show Thyself to me
My true and living God
Doing in me such works
As shall bear witness who Thou art.
Beloved of my heart
Let me so receive Thee in Thy Sacrament
That I may know what I have received
Without shadow of doubt Living bread
The very bread of life
My soul thirsts for Thee
For Thee, the living God
Leave her not hungry and thirsty, Lord
Nor dry and withered

As if it were some dead thing
She has received
Communicate to her light, love, desire
Purposes of a new life
Sorrow for her sins
A new devotion
That she may know what she has received
Not bread alone
Not a thing dead, but living
Living and life-giving
The very bread of life.
Amen.

XV. BREAD AND WINE

Most sweet Jesus
Thou didst unite Thy blessed Body
To forms of bread
That had been ground
Thy precious Blood to grapes
That had been trodden on
And passed through the press
I here offer myself to Thee
To be ground in the mill
Bruised and trodden on
Reduced even to dust
For the preservation of Thy love
And of union and concord among my brethren
Mortify the old man in me
Let me taste the sweetness
Of this divine food
Unite me to Thyself in this life

By the abundance of Thy grace
And when this life is over
In the perpetual union of glory.
Amen.

XVIII O ADMIRABILE COMMERCIUM!

My best Beloved
In giving me Thy Body
Thy most holy Flesh
Thou givest also Thy Blood
Thy soul and Thy divinity
All Thy treasures
All Thy merits and satisfactions
That I may enjoy them as my own
Thou desirest to be always with us
Our companion, our banquet
Our constant delight.
My best Beloved
How can I prove my gratitude?
Thou, Lord
Givest me the best thing Thou hast
I, therefore
Will give Thee the best thing I have
Thou dost give me Thyself
I here offer Thee myself
All that is mine
I consecrate to Thy service
My body, my blood
My life, my soul
All I can or ever may have
Help me, Lord
To fulfil this my oblation

For gratitude demands no less.
Amen.

XIX. THE HOLOCAUST

Most merciful Jesus
In this sacrament of Thy love
Thou dost give us Thy whole Body
Perfect and entire
That Thou mayest sanctify every member
Of him who receives Thee
Healing thus the whole man.
Sweet Jesus
Who hast so shrunk Thyself up in this sacrament
In order to give life to my soul
With Thine eyes and ears sanctify mine
That I may only see and hear
What is pleasing to Thine
With Thy tongue purify mine
That it speak nothing to offend Thee
With Thy hands and feet purify mine
That I may always do Thy holy will
Look upon me, my best beloved
Open the eyes of Thy mercy
That I may see Thee, know Thee
With a lively faith believe in Thee
Open Thine ears to my prayers
My sobs and my groaning
Opening mine also
That I may hear Thy word
And obey Thy holy law
Open Thy mouth
Unloose Thy blessed tongue

Speak somewhat to my heart
That my mouth may be opened to bless Thee
That my tongue may ever magnify Thee
Open, Lord, Thy breast
Enlarge the door of Thy heart
Receive me into it
Let it burn and wholly inflame me
With the fire of Thy love
Stretch forth Thy hands
Touch me with them
That mine may be sanctified
In all they do
By the steps of Thy most holy feet
Direct my steps conformably to Thine
Let my whole body be a living picture
Of that glorious sanctity and purity
With which Thine was resplendent.
Amen.

XX. PANIS VITÆ

Bread of life
Extreme of littleness
Extreme of greatness
What can be more little
Than a little crumb of this divine bread?
Yet what more great
Than God and man contained in it?
Supreme bread
Make me little
And make me great
Little in my own eyes

And great in Thine
Since Thou alone art sufficient
For millions of souls
Satisfy the desire of my soul
That henceforth I may be wholly Thine
World without end.
Amen.

XXI. CHRIST BEFORE PILATE

My soul
Dost thou not break with grief
Beholding Him thus abhorred
Who ought so greatly to be loved?
Why is thy face not bathed in tears
Beholding thy Lord's face
Swollen and bruised
Covered with spittle
Bathed with blood?
See how His enemies still thirst
To shed the rest
Even to the last drop
Love Him that so loves thee
As much as ever thou canst
Strive to make some small return
For this unjust hatred
With which He is abhorred
Wilt thou not be more fervent
In loving Him
Than His enemies were
In hating Him?
Amen.

XXII. THE FIVE WOUNDS

Most sweet Jesus
By that wonderful love
Which brings Thee to my poor dwelling
With Thy five wounds
Bestow on me I beseech Thee
These five virtues
By the two wounds of Thy sacred feet
I crave humility and meekness
By the two wounds of Thy holy hands
I beg obedience and perseverance
By the wound of Thy blessed side
Fill me with Thy burning charity
Grant me to love Thee and obey Thee
Persevering ever in Thy love
Grant me at length the crown of glory.
Amen.

XXIII. FORNAX ARDENS

Most loving Jesus
My Redeemer and my brother
Spouse of chaste souls
What shall I render Thee
For all the wounds Thou hast received
For love of me?
Sweet and tender-hearted Lover
Wound my heart
With the wounds of love and sorrow
That I may love Thee a little
Who hast so greatly loved me.
Break my heart with compassion

For all that Thou hast suffered for me.
Give me leave, Lord
To enter into the wound of Thy side
Let me be wholly inflamed
Burnt up and consumed
In this furnace of love
Which burns in Thy heart.
Amen.

XXIV. THE DEATH SENTENCE

I give Thee thanks
Most meek Redeemer
For Thy most pitiful heart
Which accepted a sentence
So unjust and cruel
To deliver me from eternal death
To which I was justly condemned
Dear Lord
How shall I repay this good will?
Behold now I give Thee my will
That it may for ever fulfil Thine.
In penance for my sins
I lovingly accept all pain or sorrow
That shall ever come to me
From Thee or from men.
Help me therefore with Thy holy grace
Let me never fail to obey Thy commands
Either through fear or timidity
Nor be found wanting in those duties
Which Thou hast laid on me.
Amen.

XXV. DIVINE LIFE

Bread of life
Quicken in me the life of Christ
Let me live no longer in myself
But in Him
Let me not live the life of man
But the life of God himself.
Divine bread
Let me so eat Thee
That henceforth I may desire only Christ
Jesus Christ and Him crucified
Let me never love or desire aught else
But only Christ
All for Christ, all by Christ,
All in Christ
Heavenly bread
Unite me to Christ
That I may live the life of God
The life of Christ united with God
As He lived the same life with His Father.
Amen.

XXVI. THE SAVIOUR'S FOUNTAINS

Sweet Saviour Christ
When I approach Thy divine sacrament
Put my lips to Thy very side
That I may drink of the water and blood
Which gushes thence
Let me share in the gifts and graces
Which flow from these Thy fountains.
Most loving Saviour

By Thy pain Thou hast merited these waters
Which I draw with joy from Thy wounds
Shut not up these channels from me
Though my ingratitude deserves it.
Henceforth I purpose by Thy grace
To run to them
Not seldom, nor lazily
But very frequently
Filling my soul with graces and virtues
To Thy honour and glory. Amen.

XXVII. THE PIERCED SIDE

God of my soul
Wound my heart with the dart of Thy charity
Through the wounds of Thy sacred body.
With that water and blood
Which came forth from Thy side
Satisfy the thirst of my soul
Wash me
Purify me
Inflame me
Let me enter in spirit
Into these glorious wounds
I desire with all my soul
To dwell within them
And within Thee
Uniting myself with Thee
By the union of love
Till I be made one with Thee
In the union of glory.
Amen.

XXVIII. A LIVING TOMB

Remember, my soul
When thou dost communicate
Thou art made the sepulchre of Christ
Receiving Him within thee
Truly alive in Himself
Though dead to outward eyes
See that thy sepulchre be glorious
Hewed out in a rock
Let it be glorious by virtues
New by renovation of spirit
Grounded in the imitation of Jesus
Who is the living rock.
Most sweet Christ
Sanctify this sepulchre
Into which Thou dost enter
Keep it worthy of Thy indwelling
As long as Thou dost remain in it.
In Thine own sepulchre
Never was any placed but Thyself.
Most gentle Lord
Who dost deign to visit this poor soul
Keep it for Thyself alone
Let nothing enter
That may displease Thee
Let no creature profane it
Preserve it ever new and pure
For Thy everlasting glory.
Amen.

XXIX. THY SEAL

Christ Jesus our Lord
Thou comest to me in Holy Communion
Making my soul Thy habitation
And Thy sepulchre
Teach me how to keep it diligently
Sealing it and guarding it
Lest any steal Thee from me
Lest I lose the spirit of devotion
What seal can I use more secure
What guard more powerful
Than Thyself?
Thou my Beloved hast said
Put Me as a seal upon thy heart
As a seal upon thy arm
For love is strong as death
Jealousy hard as Hell
Receive I pray Thee my heart
My senses and my powers
Seal them with the seal of Thy charity
The imitation of Thy glorious virtues
That sealed with this seal
I may enjoy Thee for ever.
Amen.

XXX. THE EMPTY TOMB

God of my soul
Who wert used to dwell within me
Rejoicing me with Thy blessed presence
Where art Thou now?
Who has taken Thee from me?

Who has plucked Thee from my heart?
Why dost Thou leave me alone
Dry, heavy and comfortless?
If my sins have done this
Let Thy infinite mercy cleanse me
That Thou mayest return
And dwell with me once more.
Keep my soul always clean
Fill it with Thy grace
So shall I have Thee always with me
So wilt Thou never leave me again.
Amen.

XXXI. MANE NOBISCUM DOMINE

Stay with me, good Jesus
Lest the light of faith be darkened
The splendour of virtue decline
The fervour of charity grow cold
If Thou leave me
I shall be like a cold dark night
Stay with me also Lord
My day draws towards its night
My death approaches
And I need Thy presence more
Lord Thou hast said
If anyone love Me
He will keep My word
My Father will love him
And We will come to him
And make Our abode with him
My Lord

I desire to love Thee
I promise to obey Thee
With all the affection of my heart
Stay with me Lord
That I may accomplish this desire
That I may attain to life everlasting
Where I shall abide with Thee
World without end. Amen.

XXXII. VENI DOMINE

Most sweet Redeemer
When Thou didst leave this world
Thou didst say to Thy apostles
I will come again
And will take you to Myself
That where I am
You also may be.
Come, I beseech Thee
Visit my soul
Fill it with Thy grace
In virtue of Thy sacrament of union
Bring me where Thou art;
There may I see
What here I believe
There may I possess
What here I hope for;
Let me enjoy Thy divine presence
World without end.
Amen.

XXXIII. PIGNUS FUTURÆ GLORIÆ

Tree of life
Placed in the Paradise of God
Pledge of immortality
And of life eternal
Give me to eat of Thy most sweet fruit
Preserve my soul from all kinds of death
Vitalise it with all kinds of life
Poor soul of mine
If thou desire eternal life
Feed in spirit on this divine food
The pledge and source of it
Poor body
If thou desire to rise again
To the life of eternal bliss
Feed on this precious body
Assured pledge of thy resurrection
And of the life of glory promised thee.
Amen.

XXXIV. I STAND AT THE DOOR AND KNOCK

Sovereign Prince
Vouchsafe to enter this poor habitation
To sup with me
But bring with Thee the supper
Thou delightest to eat
On my part
I offer myself
To prepare the same
In the best manner I am able.
Amen.

XXXV. SUPER OMNIA ET IN OMNIBUS

Beloved of my soul
If Thou lovest me as Thine
I say to Thee
That I love Thee as mine
For as I am Thine
So Thou art mine
I am Thy creature
Thy slave and Thy son
Thou art my Creator
My Redeemer
My Lord and my Father
Therefore will I love Thee
Not as myself but above myself
Above all things that are created
Or are yet to be created
For Thou art worthy to be loved
More than all things soever.
Amen.

XXXVI. THE MEASURE OF LOVE

Eternal Lover
Let me love Thee with my whole heart
Mortifying all other love
Thy love alone shall remain in it
Let me love Thee with my whole will
Denying all other wills
Thy will alone shall reign in it
Let me love Thee with my whole soul
Bridling my passions and appetites
Thy love shall possess me utterly

Let me love Thee with my whole mind
Renouncing my own judgement
Subduing my understanding in obedience to faith
Fulfilling Thy will
Let me love Thee with all my strength
Mortifying my senses
Applying my powers to keep Thy law.
Since Thy behests are not impossible
Give me power to love Thee
As Thou desirest to be loved
Make that sweet and easy to me by grace
Which is impossible to my weak nature.
Amen.

XXXVII. THE GREAT COMMANDMENT

My Beloved
I desire to love Thee
As Thy love hath commanded
With my whole heart
With my whole soul
With all my strength
Without any bound or limit.
I aspire to the perfection of that love
With which a creature may love his Creator.
I desire to love Thee
More than Angels or Seraphim
Even with infinite love
A love that would never grow weary
So that I might at length attain
To that end for which Thou hast made me
Which is no other than Thyself.
Amen.

XXXVIII. DEUS MEUS, MISERICORDIA MEA

My God and my glory
What shall I say of Thy mercy?
How shall I praise Thee for it?
How may I become its vessel?
How be made its instrument?
Thy mercy had compassion on me
Before I was;
It created me
That I might be;
It goes before me
That I may work for Thee;
It accompanies me
While I am working
It surrounds me with blessings
Crowns me with victories
And gives me confidence
That in the end I shall obtain Thee.
Deus meus, misericordia mea
My God, my mercy
Thou art mercy itself
All mercy is Thine
Thou art merciful by Thy very nature
Yet mercy is mine also
For I am full of miseries
Which mercy alone can relieve.
My God, my mercy
Unite me with Thyself
In Thine eternal glory
Where Thou mayest always be mine
As I shall be thine
There let me enjoy Thy happiness

There let me be free from all misery
World without end. Amen.

XXXIX. SOLI DEO

My God, my glory
When shall I see Thee so clearly
That all my desires shall be fulfilled?
When shall my soul be made so pure
That I may see Thy divine face?
Take to Thee, Lord, all my powers
Employ them in that glorious work
Even now
Which will be theirs for ever.
Let my mind be always busied
In beholding Thee
My will
In loving Thee
My tongue
In blessing Thee
My senses and all my members
In obeying Thee
Let them all rejoice in Thee
Of Thee
For Thee
World without end. Amen.

XL. FRIENDSHIP WITH GOD

Lift up, my soul
Lift up the wings of thy heart
Above all that is created
Above thyself also

Pass from all reward
All pain or profit
Fly with swiftness to thy Creator
Love Him because He loves thee
Because He desires thy love
Give Him all He asks
It is for Thy sake
He desires it.
Praise Him and glorify Him
As much as ever thou canst
Who has commanded thee to love Him
Who gives thee strength to fulfil
What He has deigned to command
My Beloved
What is it to Thee
That I should love Thee?
What matters it to Thee
To have love and friendship with me?
It concerns me only, Lord,
Not Thee at all
Yet Thy love solicits me
As if the gain were wholly Thine.
Would I could imitate this love
By forgetting myself utterly
Then would I love Thee alone
My chief and only good
To whom be honour and glory
World without end.
Amen.

SOME SPIRITUAL MAXIMS FOUND AMONG THE PAPERS OF FR. LOUIS DE PONTE AFTER HIS DEATH

1. Do for God what thou canst, and God will do for thee what thou canst not.

2. Be faithful in little things and God will help thee to perform great ones.

3. Take the sweet things of this world as bitter and the bitter things as sweet; thus thou shalt enjoy peace.

4. Think of God and God will think of thee.

5. Be generous to thy neighbour and God will be generous to thee.

6. Give to God what He asks of thee and He will give thee what thou askest of Him.

7. If thou wishest to do the will of God, why negligently perform a duty of obedience, under pretext of passing on to something else, since thou hast in reality what thou seekest?

8. In me is nothing; in God is all.

9. I am what I am not; God is what He is.

10. True love seeks to love rather than to know, and esteems obedience more than knowledge.

10. Choose for the companions of thy life poverty, contempt and pain, because these were the chosen companions of Jesus.

11. Whatever occupations thou mayest have, endeavour to do each action with as much perfection, peace and composure as if thou hadst nothing else to do.

12. Mortify eagerness to finish one action in order to pass quickly to another, and also any and every immoderate desire, unless thou wishest thy work to be ill done.

13. What hast thou given to God, or what hast thou done for Him, that thou shouldst dare to complain when He does

not give thee what thou wishest?

14. If thou desirest always to think of God, study to forget thyself.

15. God will think of thee if thou forgettest thyself.

16. To forget oneself, is to be unmindful of honours, conveniences, life, health, consolations, spiritual delights, and whatever concerns one's own interests, except inasmuch as God wills us to remember them for His service, and for His own great glory.

17. Give more study to mortification than to contemplation, because an unmortified person seeks the spirit of prayer but cannot find it, while prayer itself seeks him who is truly mortified, and knows how to find him.

18. Leave a letter begun when God calls thee, because it is better to leave a letter well begun than badly finished.

19. God rearranges when obedience deranges thy ideas, and the action thou art about.

20. We act as God does when we do good with peace and without perturbation; with love, without self-interest; with magnanimity, without presumption.

www.ingramcontent.com/pod-product-compliance
Lightning Source LLC
Chambersburg PA
CBHW030255010526
44107CB00053B/1715